CW00536305

'JUST A 𝚒ALKER'

'JUST A TALKER'

The Sayings of Dr John Duncan

Selected and Edited by

John M. Brentnall

'Why do *you* not write a book?'
'I cannot write, I'm just a talker.'

THE BANNER OF TRUTH TRUST

THE BANNER OF TRUTH TRUST
3 Murrayfield Road, Edinburgh EH12 6EL
P.O.Box 621, Carlisle, Pennsylvania 17013, USA

*

© John M.Brentnall 1997
First Published 1997
ISBN 0 85151 7269

*

Typeset at The Spartan Press Ltd,
Lymington, Hants
Printed in Finland by
WSOY – Book Printing Division

To Elsa,

Alison and Mike,

Jonathan and Kathleen,

and

All the Christian Friends

at

Derwent Free Church, Chaddesden, Derby

CONTENTS

PREFACE   xv

BIOGRAPHICAL INTRODUCTION   xvii
by John E. Marshall and John J. Murray

SOME LEADING ASPECTS OF DR DUNCAN'S LIFE   xxxiv

PART I: SHORTER SAYINGS

Adoption	3
Affliction	3
Angels	4
Antinomianism	4
Arminianism	5
Assurance of Salvation	6
Atheism	7
Atonement	8
Baptism	9
Bible	10
Bible Characters	16
Books	19
Brethrenism	19
Calvinism	20
Christ	21
Christianity	39
Church	39

Church Government	42
The Church in Scotland	43
Civil Government and Rulers	43
Comfort	44
Conscience	44
Controversy	47
Conversion	48
Conviction of Sin	51
Creation	51
Creatures	52
Creeds and Confessions of Faith	53
Death	53
Despondency	56
Devils or Demons	56
Devotion to God	57
Doctrine	57
Doubts and Doubting	58
Duty	60
Election	60
The English Language	61
Envy and Vaunting	61
Evangelicalism	62
Evangelism	62
Experience	62
Faith	62
Family Worship	67
Fasting	68
Fear	68
Feelings	68
Flattery	68
Free Will	68
Friendship	69

Contents

Genius	69
Glory	70
God	70
Godliness	84
Goodness	84
Good Works	85
Gospel	85
Grace	91
Hatred	93
Heart	93
Heaven	94
Hell	95
History	96
Holiness	96
The Holy Spirit	96
Hope	97
Humility	97
Hyper-Calvinists	98
Hypocrisy and Hypocrites	98
Idolatry	99
Intolerance	99
Jews	99
Joy	101
Justification	102
Kindness	103
Kings and Priests	104
Knowledge	104
Language and Languages	104
Law	105
Life	109
Lord's Day	110
Lord's Supper	110

Love	112
Man	115
Marriage and Divorce	118
Means of Grace	119
Merit	119
Ministers and Ministry	120
Miracles and the Miraculous	122
Music in Worship	123
Mysticism	124
Nature and Natural Blessings	125
Non-Essentials	125
Obedience and Disobedience	125
Old Testament Saints	126
Order	127
Pantheism	127
Peace	128
Pelagianism	128
Perdition	129
Perfectionism	129
Perseverance of the Saints	129
Philosophers and Thinkers	130
Philosophies	132
Philosophy	133
Pleasure	133
Poetry and Poets	134
Praise	134
Prayer	135
Preaching	139
Predestination	141
Pride	141
Progress	142
Promises of God	143

Contents

Property and Possession	144
Protestants	144
Providence	144
Psalms	145
Redemption	147
Regeneration	147
Regulative Principle	149
Religion	149
Repentance	151
Revelation	153
Revival	153
Roman Catholicism	154
Salvation	155
Sanctification	157
Sandemanianism	158
Satan	158
Science	159
Self-Examination	159
Self-Expression	160
Self-Fulfilment	160
Self-Sufficiency	160
Sin	160
Sincerity	169
Singing in Worship	169
Speculation	170
Spiritual Frames and Conditions	170
Supernatural	172
Theologians	172
Theology	184
Trust	185
Truth	185
Unbelief	185

Will   186
Women   186
World   187
Worship   189

PART II: LONGER EXTRACTS

Anthems   193
Assurance   193
Believers   202
Christ   203
Communion of Saints   211
Conscience   213
Conversion   213
Death   214
Debt   216
Effectual Calling   217
Establishment Principle   222
Extermination of the Canaanites   223
Faith   224
God   225
Gospel   227
The Holy Spirit   230
Jews   232
Justification   233
Law   236
Love   242
Man   245
Ministry   246
Obedience   247
Passion Week   249
Preaching   249

Contents

Prophets	255
Psalms, Paraphrases and Hymns	255
Semi-Pelagianism and Arminianism	256
Sin	256
Sincerity	261
Theology	262
Threefold Union	265
EPILOGUE	266
BIBLIOGRAPHY	267
INDEX	269

PREFACE

The spiritual firmament of the Free Church of Scotland at the time of the Disruption in 1843 was adorned with a galaxy of stars – men possessing much grace, eminent gifts and tireless energy in the service of Christ. They were burning and shining lights, in whose holy radiance thousands of God's people loved to walk. One of these stars was Dr John Duncan, affectionately known as 'Rabbi' Duncan on account of his thorough acquaintance with everything Jewish. 'Even his jokes at times were absurdly Hebraic,' said David Brown. But it is as a Christian, supremely, that Duncan speaks to us today for he was a believer with profound thoughts, vast learning, deep humility, intense spirituality and exclusive devotion to the Lord Jesus Christ.

Although Duncan was a master of the English language (as well as many others), and had a wonderful sense of the music of words, he never wrote a book. When an acquaintance once found him absorbed in a volume on Job he asked him, 'Why do *you* not write a book?' 'I cannot write,' he replied, 'I'm just a talker.' 'A road to walk on,' said another, 'a subject of importance to speak about, a friend to talk to – these were evidently all he wanted, with occasionally a hearty pinch of snuff.' Dr Duncan, said John Macleod in 1943, 'had a genius for epigrammatic wisdom', and 'though he left next to nothing in writing there are some books in which so much of his teaching is treasured up and preserved; and there are scarcely any books of this generation in Scotland that are even yet more greedily sought after than these.'

What I have sought to do in these pages is take the aphorisms of his conversations, as recorded in several original sources[1] and present them here in one book, believing that they will greatly enrich the hearts and minds of all who read them.

The amount of clear thought packed into these pages is altogether out of proportion to their number. Duncan's sayings have a near unique combination of depth and brevity. He exemplified the standard he expected of others: 'I would advise everyone to be very careful to use no more words than are necessary to express thought. Whenever a man becomes cloudy in his words, be sure that his thought has become shadowy too.' On Duncan's death, William Knight remarked, 'With him has perished a breathing library of wisdom.' But through the efforts of Knight and others this book will show that much of lasting value remains.

Finally, thanks are due to the Rev. John J. Murray and the Rev. John E. Marshall for their willingness for some of the material they wrote on Duncan in the Banner of Truth magazine some years ago to be used here as a Biographical Introduction.

John M. Brentnall
November 1996

---

[1]These are listed in the bibliography, p. 267 below. I am especially indebted to William Knight's *Colloquia Peripatetica* (Edinburgh, 1870).

BIOGRAPHICAL INTRODUCTION

'During the quarter of a century which ended in 1870, there might have been seen almost daily in the streets of Edinburgh, during the winter months, an old man of singular appearance and mien; short of stature, and spare of figure, with head unusually bent, and eye that either dropped or gazed wistfully abroad, as if recognising a reality behind the illusions of sense; the expression of his face one of lonely abstraction, with lines indicative of many a struggle with the darker side of things; more like an apparition from a mediaeval cloister, than a man of the 19th century. His pathetic look and generally uncouth appearance were sure to attract the notice of the passer-by.' That man so graphically described by Professor William Knight was the altogether original and unique Dr John Duncan, professor of Hebrew in the New College, Edinburgh.

John Duncan was born in 1796 in Aberdeen. His father was a shoemaker and John the only surviving child of the marriage between his father and Ann Mutch who also came from near Aberdeen. His mother died when he was still young, and his father married again. His stepmother was a great blessing to him and he regarded her with affection till the end of her life. Both John's parents were members of the Secession Church. One of Duncan's biographers describes his father as 'a detached boulder of granite, hard and solitary . . . an upright man, walking in the fear of God, strict in his Secession principles, rugged and stern, in family discipline inexorable.'

John was sent to Grammar School and then to the University in Aberdeen. While at University, in spite of the strictness of his upbringing, and in spite, no doubt, of the excellent teaching he received in the Secession Church, he lapsed into complete atheism, denying the existence of God, of angelic spirit and of the human soul. Strange though it may seem, we know that in 1813 Duncan offered himself for examination and was accepted as a student of Divinity in the Constitutional Associate Presbytery of the Secession Church. In 1816, however, he left the Secession and joined the Established Church of Scotland. Duncan himself gave very little information about the reasons for this change and therefore the thinking which led up to it is shrouded in a certain mystery. What we do have is his testimony to his condition at the time when he entered the Divinity Hall of the Established Church: 'I was an atheist when I entered Dr Mearns' Class. I had a godly upbringing, but I broke off from it. I had three years of dreary atheism and during that time I made a doctrinal atheist of a pupil of mine who died.'

This atheism could not fail to affect his life and there is no doubt that it was associated with an inevitable bondage to sin and with a fearful sense of intellectual desolation. In describing his condition at this time he frequently repeated in later years the words from the dream of a man called John Paul: 'I wandered to the furthest verge of Creation, and there I saw a Socket where an Eye should have been and I heard the shriek of a Fatherless World.'

But God had purposes of grace and mercy for this deluded sinner. His recovery from error was not to be rapid; indeed while, as we shall see, his conversion was sudden and drastic, yet the processes that led up to it were slow. It was through the teaching of Dr Duncan Mearns that he was led out of his atheism into an intellectual acceptance of the existence of God. Duncan himself described what happened to him: 'I first saw clearly the existence of God in walking along the bridge at Aberdeen; it was a great discovery to me; I stopped and stood in an ecstasy of joy at seeing the existence of God. When I was convinced that there was a God, I danced on the Brig o' Dee with delight'.

Yet his recovery from error was, as we have said, a lengthy process. While now relinquishing his atheism, he became a Sabellian, that is to say, he held the view of Sabellius that the Father, Son and Holy Ghost are not three distinct personal subsistences in the one Godhead, but only three modes or manifestations of the one personality in the Godhead. His condition at this time is well described by David Brown:

Henceforward for a period of nine years, Mr Duncan was little troubled with theological difficulties, and concerned himself but little about his spiritual state – indeed, scarcely about his moral reputation. In theism he was so established as never to have his belief again shaken; and having soon after become convinced of the truth of Divine revelation, he was never again seriously disturbed on that head. Yet so unsubdued was his intellectual pride, as long afterwards he confessed to myself, that he resolved to 'stand out against all doctrines'. [He was] . . . untroubled by any questions about the Divinity of Christ, the Atonement and other peculiar doctrines of the Gospel. In this generalized Christianity he found little to trouble his conscience, and nothing to control his wayward will, while the fear of damnation – strong at first as a feeling – got so reduced by habitual disregard of its voice, as to amount to nothing beyond the mere intellectual result of a readjusted theology.

Duncan was at this time according to his own confession living without prayer and in habitual sin. In this condition in 1825 he took licence to preach, having held back from this step for a long time. Speaking of this many years later he said, 'I took licence in unbelief, in ungodliness and doctrinal unbelief and heresy.' On being asked how the authorities allowed him to pass when his views were such he replied, 'Because I was a hypocrite, not willingly, for I kept back for long; but at last the people were upon me, and out of very shame I acted the hypocrite; I did not choose to tell them why I was not taking licence.'

It was about this same time that David Brown, Duncan's friend and future biographer, came to an experimental knowledge of evangelical truth. Being in Edinburgh at this time, Brown came under the influence of César Malan, who was on a mission to this country. Malan's remarkable zeal for souls, his pressing men and women for an immediate decision, and the wonderful effect of his methods deepened Brown's evangelical convictions and filled him with a passionate desire to deal on the same principles with Duncan. Malan was expected to visit Aberdeen, so on his return there David Brown sought out his old friend hoping to prepare him for a possible meeting with Malan. 'I was in a very softened state of mind when I met Malan,' said Duncan in after-life. He was referring to a six-hour-long duel with David

Brown as they paced the Aberdeen streets in front of Duncan's lodgings. Duncan professed his belief in a personal God but stated quite emphatically, 'the doctrines I can't and won't believe, I mean the Divinity and Atonement of Christ . . . To tell you the truth, the words "heaven" and "hell" sound in my ears with as little effect as the words "tables" and "chairs". And yet I do sometimes feel a little.' To which Brown replied, 'What you feel is not the question. What I want you to tell me is, Are you holy?' This sentence struck a wounding blow and the labour bestowed by David Brown was soon to be reaped by another hand.

The very contrast between César Malan – quick, incisive, dogmatic – and Duncan – questioning, philosophical, 'naturally of a sceptical turn of mind' – fitted them for each other when God's hour had come. 'He was the first gentlemanly intellectual and altogether pleasant dogmatist I had met,' says Duncan. Malan's method in personal dealing was this: he invariably used the text 'Whosoever believeth that Jesus is the Christ is born of God' (1 *John* 5:1) and pressed the question on the hearer, 'Do you believe that Jesus is the Christ?' If the answer was 'Yes', the conclusion was 'then you are born of God'. This syllogism – by which, Duncan believed afterwards, 'he did much good and some harm' – was tried on the young sceptic, but he fought against it. 'At last in our talk,' says Duncan, 'I happened to be quoting a text. He started forward and said, "See! You have the Word of God in your mouth." It passed through me like electricity – the great thought that God *meant* man to know *His* mind: God – His Word – in my very mouth. It was, I believe, the seed of perhaps all I have.' Certain it was that his 'philosophical pride' received its death blow. Henceforward the Scriptures were God's voice to his soul and he submitted to them entirely. This was the keynote of the remarkable experience of which he said, 'that was crushed up into a moment which it would take long to unfold'.[1] Two days later, 'as I sat down to study', continues Duncan, 'and took my pen in my hand, I became suddenly the passive recipient of all the truths which I heard and had been taught in my childhood. I sat there unmoving for hours and they came and preached themselves to me.'

The evidence of a change was unmistakable. He was full of 'joy and peace in believing' and in his zeal so pressed salvation on all that an old minister likened him to 'a policeman arresting people on the streets at night', and compelling them to come in. The influence of his 'spiritual father' was evident in the prominence given to the immediate duty of believing and the stress laid on a high and instant assurance. 'I began to preach high assurance', he said to a friend in later life, 'I preached things about Christ, about the Trinity, about sin, about the Incarnation, about the Atonement; and I thought I was warranted to preach that people who believed that were regenerated: I thought I was warranted to preach assurance on that ground. That was the defect of Malanism.'

For about two years this high assurance lasted. Gradually,

---

[1]Referring at a later date to his change of views with regard to the Christian Revelation he said, 'When I gave up my sceptical opinions I did not pick them out one by one, but I *got a vomit and vomited them all up*. I might have attended more to the Apologetic had I picked them out bit by bit, but I threw up my speculations, and admitted the Bible just at once.'

however, the joy and confidence which resulted from his conversion experience passed away, though Duncan continued to hold them forth as the normal condition of the Christian. He became increasingly aware that there must be something wrong, though as yet he knew not what. The evidence of a change of views was seen in the meeting David Brown and he held from seven to eight in the morning to awaken interest in truths hitherto kept too much in the background. But his difficulties only increased. To quote his own account of it near the close of his life, 'By and by, all that began in sincerity went away and I continued preaching assurance when the thing was gone. But at last the hypocrisy became utterly intolerable, and then I humbly think the Spirit took a strong dealing with me.' 'The inflated air-vessel,' comments Moody Stuart, 'was pierced, and fell in with a terrible collapse. He fell into darkness, doubt, fear, all but absolute despair. He lost utterly all confidence in the past, had not one spark of light for the present, and only a ray of hope for the future.'

In this experience, which Duncan came to call his 'second conversion', he went through what the Reformers and Puritans liked to call a 'law work'. This conflict brought him into a new realm of doctrinal and experimental truth. His gradual recovery out of this distress is best told in his own words:

'I came to see that God had a Covenant of Grace, and that this Covenant embraced a salvation that is suited to my *case* but said nothing about my *person*. From that I came to the Mediator of the Covenant, and the Person and Offices of Christ, and I saw a Saviour suited to me. Then I took a step further. My attention was at this time in great measure directed to the Person of Christ – it was a matter of life and death with me – to the sufficiency of Christ in His offices and work for the chief of sinners; and to this, that He was freely offered to me in the gospel; that the command of God was that I should receive Him, and that the commination[1] of God was a tremendously additional condemnation above that of the law, and the justice of that, because I had no right to reject Christ – no right to be damned.'

We break the quotation here to point out the connection between Duncan's thought and experience at this time and the writings of John Owen and Herman Witsius, which he described as having a special influence on him. Witsius was one of the fullest and most exact expositors of federal or covenant theology – the systematic arrangement of biblical truth under the covenant of works and covenant of grace – and his work *The Economy of the Covenants* shaped Duncan's thought on the subject. Owen, of the same school as Witsius, appealed to Duncan chiefly for his rich spiritual works on *The Person and Glory of Christ* and on *The Holy Spirit*.

It is not surprising that in the midst of this spiritual upheaval Duncan doubted the reality of his 'first conversion', and even the validity of the views of truth formerly held. It seemed indeed as if the foundation was being re-laid, and in a sense that is what took place. The first foundation was true but it required to be laid deeper. Thereafter he remained suspicious of any superficial assurance of salvation, and suspicious, most of all, of himself.

In 1830 Duncan removed to his first pastorate at Persie, a country parish in Perthshire. His stay there was brief but

---

[1]That is, the threatening of divine vengeance.

he showed a great love for the people and afterwards spoke highly of their capacity to listen to well-argued sermons. In 1831 he was called to Glasgow, first to a lectureship in Duke Street Gaelic Chapel, and then, in 1836, to the ministry at Milton Chapel. Whilst he was there he married a Miss Janet Tower of Aberdeen. She was a choice character of eminent godliness and his marriage was very happy. Perhaps it was characteristic of the man that during their courtship, which of course had to be carried on largely by letter, he set himself to teach her Greek. 'He covers his paper with Greek inflexions in bold characters, illustrates this by a comparison with the structure of Latin, crosses his writing, and fills with compact sentences every quarter of an inch of space in the margins and corners of the quarto pages'. He worries whether he is trying her too much and so breaks off into French! She obviously was a woman of great ability, and perhaps of tact as well, for she replies, 'As for Greek, I find your notes very interesting and very helpful to me. You make the thing appear simpler to me and more easy to be attained than I at first supposed.'

In 1838 they had a daughter, Anne. Early in 1839 Mrs Duncan gave birth to another child, but shatteringly for Duncan the child only survived a few minutes and Mrs Duncan for a few days. As has been observed, these experiences prepared him to be a son of consolation to many. Referring to the tenderness of his preaching, a Glasgow woman once said, 'Oh, he was rale merciful.' Later Duncan remarried, his second wife being a widow and also a woman of great worth. Two daughters were born to them, Annie and Maria.[1] After her decease in

---

[1] Maria married the Rev. Mr Spaeth, a Lutheran pastor in Philadelphia, in 1865. They had two sons, John and Douglas.

1852 Duncan had two excellent housekeepers, Miss Sanderson and Miss Robertson, women of sterling character and piety who were a great boon to a man who really was quite incapable of looking after himself.

It was at this time that there was a reviving of interest in work among the Jews. A group of men was sent out to survey the situation, among them Robert Murray M'Cheyne. They travelled extensively in Europe and the near East and returned to give a report to the Church. At the same time Duncan had applied for the Chair of Oriental Languages in Glasgow but was unsuccessful. In July 1840 he was appointed first missionary to the Jews from the Church of Scotland. In June 1841 he left Scotland for his chosen field of labour which was Budapest. This was one of the happier periods of his life. By his encyclopaedic knowledge of Hebrew and Jewish literature and his eminent personal piety he gained ready access to the Jews. In due time many Jews were converted, among them some who would attain to eminence as Christians. These were times of a great working by the Spirit. Duncan's coming was instrumental in much blessing to the Hungarian Reformed Church and a new flowering of spiritual life among the Protestant churches in Hungary. Adolph Saphir (a Jewish convert) wrote thus to Dr Keith of the fruit of Dr Duncan's influence: 'The first time you were here there was not a village in all Hungary in which they knew there was such a thing as Evangelical religion. The second time you were here [in 1844] there was not a village in all Hungary in which they did not know; and now there is not a presbytery in Hungary in which the Gospel is not preached.'

It is possible to speculate that Dr Duncan might have

been happier had he continued in this work for which he was so eminently suited. In 1843 there took place the Disruption in the Church of Scotland and like his fellow missionaries Dr Duncan threw in his lot with the Free Church. He then received a unanimous call to the Chair of Hebrew in the Free Church of Scotland College – 'New College' – in Edinburgh which he accepted and it was in this work that he continued through the remaining twenty-seven years of his life. He also continued active in the general work of the Church, particularly at Free St Luke's, Queen Street, Edinburgh, where he served as an elder under the Rev. A. Moody Stuart and 'was long one of the spiritual factors and forces'.[1] In Moody Stuart's biography, written by his son and published in 1899, Alexander Whyte recalled one of his own memories of a communion service at St Luke's:

> I see your father over thirty-four years as he walked about the pulpit floor that morning with his pocket Bible in his hand, and with his rich mind and deep heart welling up over all his week's preparation, and making it all so fresh, so spontaneous, so contagious, so soul-quickening to us all. I see Dr Duncan, now laughing, now weeping, all the time, and all the rest of us in the same state of mind.[2]

In the 1860s Duncan helped to establish a new Free Church congregation in the Grange area of Edinburgh and, while he and Moody Stuart remained life-long friends, he transferred to Chalmers Memorial Church (as

---

[1]*Alexander Moody Stuart: A Memoir, partly autobiographical*, K. Moody Stuart (Hodder and Stoughton: London, 1899), p. 94.
[2]*Ibid.*, pp. 358–9.

it came to be named) when Horatius Bonar became its first minister in 1866. The proximity of the new church to his own home on the south side of the city was undoubtedly the principal reason for this change.

By this date Duncan's years of usefulness were almost over. On January 1, 1868, he wrote:

> *So glorious a thought should cheer*
> *Drooping hearts, and banish fear,*
> *Our battle against sin*
> *He'll end, who did begin:*
> *His mighty help alone*
> *We implore.*
>
> *Till our Lord again appear,*
> *His heavenly voice let us hear;*
> *That the vict'ry o'er sin*
> *By His grace we may win,*
> *And be where He is gone,*
> *Evermore.*

A little over two years later, on February 26, 1870, he entered the world where sin and death are no more.

It remains to say a little of John Duncan's influence as a teacher of divinity. That he had the potential qualifications for a successful Professor of Hebrew no one can doubt; that his capacity did not materialize in the duties of his office is generally acknowledged. His mind according to one of his former students was 'by far the freshest, subtlest, most original and suggestive' in the faculty of the New College. He had an omnivorous intellectual appetite and his powers of retention were vast. His attainments in learning were such as led a German student to say, 'The Germans study one thing, and know it thoroughly; the Scotch have a smattering of everything, and know nothing well; but there is one man in Scotland, John Duncan, who knows everything, and he knows them all better than we know any one.' As regards Hebrew language and literature, scarce any man knew his subject so well or loved it so much. Moreover, Duncan was passionately fond of sharing his knowledge with others.

These endowments, however, were counteracted by certain weaknesses which hindered his usefulness. There was a lack of any plan in his acquisition of knowledge. He had a fatal tendency to miscellaneousness. He was often carried away intellectually with some engrossing mental problem or absorbed spiritually with some enquiry into the state of his own soul. Furthermore, he was utterly unmethodical in everything but the arrangement of his thoughts. The greatest defect of his character, however, was, as Dr Moody Stuart points out, weakness of purpose. 'You could not name any living man whom you could so easily turn aside in judgment from what he had approved, or in execution from what he had intended.' This irregularity in work was fatal to his potential power as a professor and scholar. In this realm he was rather a great possibility than a great realization.

Whatever his defects as a professor, his position in the Hebrew chair gave him an audience and his particular talents found their natural outlet. The type of work which he did in an irregular manner could never have been done by a more symmetrical and academic instructor. Students who were aware of his limitations as a professor nevertheless realised the incalculable advantage and privilege of coming under his influence. Intellectually, theologically, exegetically and spiritually they received great benefit from 'the Rabbi', as he was felicitously called by them, and the thought and life of many future ministers, who in turn would influence others, were possibly moulded more by Duncan than by any of his fellow professors.

If he did not accomplish much by academic discourse he certainly did by his marvellous conversational powers. 'His realm was colloquial,' says A. Taylor Innes. 'But in that realm it seemed as if Pascal had shuffled into the sandals of Socrates and walked up and down our Edinburgh streets, with a large utterance of response to the inquiring youth around.'[1] He was to his students a peripatetic teacher of wisdom. As one of Duncan's colleagues at Budapest put it: 'If our staid forms of theological training had admitted of his being turned, along with his students, at a given hour twice a week, into the Princes Street Gardens, there to walk, talk and discuss in perfect freedom – content sometimes to get nothing, at other times obtaining glimpses into vistas of thought sufficient to last a lifetime – there would have been inaugurated the greatest school of theological learning in modern Europe.' He needed the stimulus of a living presence to bring the best out of him and 'while he wrote little on paper, he wrote much on living minds, in spoken words full of light and fire'.

The study of theology to him was not merely abstract and academic but something which captivated his whole being. He believed that without a personal experience of

[1] *Studies in Scottish History* (London, 1892), p. 183.

sin and grace, Christian theology was unintelligible and unreal. A striking example of what he was in this respect as a teacher is found in the *Recollections* by Moody Stuart. It is the eye-witness account of one of Duncan's students and is worthy of reproduction in full. The professor was reading a part of Isaiah, which dealt with the sufferings of the Messiah, with his senior class when his mind became engrossed with the subject and

bent nearly double, was pacing up and down in front of the students' benches, his snuff box and pocket-handkerchief in one hand, a huge pinch of snuff occupying the fingers of the other, but utterly forgotten in the absorbing interest of his subject, our Lord's sufferings for sinners, which he was turning over and looking at, now on this side, now on that, but all with a loving reverence, and as one who spoke in a half-sleeping vision, when suddenly a flash went through him as if heaven had opened. He straightened himself up, his face kindled into a rapture, his hand went up and the snuff scattered itself from his unconscious fingers as he turned to the class, more as it seemed for sympathy than to teach – 'Ay, ay, d'ye know what it was – dying on the cross, forsaken by His Father – d'ye know what it was? What? What? (As if somebody had given him a *half* answer which stimulated him, but which he had to clear out of his way, a very usual exclamation of his when wrapped in thought.) What? What? It was damnation – and damnation taken *lovingly*'. And he subsided into his chair, leaning a little to one side, his head very straight and stiff, his arms hanging down on either side beyond the arms of his chair, with the light beaming from his face and tears trickling down his cheeks he repeated in a low intense voice that broke into a half sob, half laugh in the middle, 'It was damnation – and he took it *lovingly.'* No saying of the many I have heard from him, nothing in all his manner and expression, ever struck me like this.[1]

Making allowances for Duncan's eccentricities, could anything be more fitted to impress the truth on young minds? How far removed this is from the 'orthodox' forms of divinity training with which we have become familiar can be easily judged. He presented to his students, as one of them put it, 'a living embodiment of deep, exercised, spiritual religion'. His very presence was a living influence for good. 'The more abundant presence of God', he would say, 'may be expected in a theological school where there are a good many of genuine piety.'

John Duncan many not have quite filled the place that was expected of him in academic circles and it would appear that he made no lasting contribution to theological learning, yet as Professor Knight says, no one could look upon him 'without feeling that he presented to his students a better, because a living, evidence of the supernatural than the apologetic treatises which other men wrote'.

We conclude with this striking summary of Duncan's character as a Christian, written by Moody Stuart:

Jesus Christ, in his person, his character, his life and his death, was the central subject of his thoughts, and increasingly year by year till the end. It was not theology but Christ that filled both his mind and his heart; the whole

---

[1]*Recollections of the late John Duncan*, A. Moody Stuart (Edmonston and Douglas: Edinburgh, 1872), pp. 104-5. Reprinted as *The Life of John Duncan* (Banner of Truth: Edinburgh, 1991). This is a fragrant, spiritual book though the *Life* by David Brown (Edmonston and Douglas: Edinburgh, 1872) remains the principal biography.

stress of his theology sprang from him as its source and flowed to him as its ocean. The holy Lord God of his earlier years was his fear and delight to the last, and it was ever true of him that 'he feared God above many', but in the latter portion of his life Jesus Christ was peculiarly the one object of his desires and the constant subject of his meditation.

This interest in Christ rose above every passing interest of earth. In the questions of the day he took a lively concern; not in party politics, on which I never heard him utter a word in the midst of all his talk, but in all subjects of national welfare. A friend met him in the street at a time of some public interest, and not in mere fun asked him, 'Is there any news today?' 'Oh, yes,' he replied, 'this is always news, the blood of Jesus Christ cleanseth us from all sin'.

John E. Marshall
John J. Murray

SOME LEADING ASPECTS
OF DR DUNCAN'S LIFE

His Place in Christian History

'One of the most remarkable men of this or of any other age.'

David Brown

'More than any man I ever knew, he trusted every word, reverenced every word, and loved every word in the book of God.'

A. Moody Stuart

'If you have got any good from me, you owe it all to that remarkable man of God, Dr Duncan, of Edinburgh.'

William C. Burns, preaching in Perth

'He seemed to be a child and a giant in one – both characters curiously intermingled, making intercourse with him peculiarly delightful. No man ever inspired less awe, nor called forth deeper reverence.'

R. Smith

'In him . . . the Patristic, the Scholastic and the Puritan were finely blended.'

William Knight

Some Leading Aspects of Dr Duncan's Life

As a Conversationalist

'His language was concise, oracular and singularly beautiful; every word was a thought, sought out as a jewel and fitted artistically in its place.'

A. Moody Stuart

'He seemed to me to have embodied the results of his thoughts on most subjects in compendious sentences and aphorisms, which were always ready whenever he had occasion to speak on any given subject.'

James J. Smith

'He strove to give his thoughts a certain chaste beauty of form: some of his characteristic sayings, through being often repeated, became almost perfect in point of form.'

R. J. Sandeman

'He had a fastidious sense of the music of words.'

A. Moody Stuart

'His sayings, aided by their epigrammatic terseness and point, stuck fast in the conscience and memory, in their measure, like texts of Scripture.'

John Donaldson

'His thoughts naturally took an aphoristic form; and sometimes they were less utterances for others than audible soliloquy. But brevity and sententious fulness always characterised them.'

William Knight

'One knows not whether most to wonder at the range of ancient and modern literature which he swept over in these conversations, the critical grasp which he took of every subject and every leading book which came up for talk, the profound and beautiful thoughts to which they gave birth or the consummate mastery of the English tongue which even in talk he displayed.'

David Brown

His Love for Others

'When he wearied of his books, he loved to relax himself in frolic with young children. He had the manhood that becomes to the child a child. Children soon came to look upon him as one of themselves.'

David Brown

'Speaking of G.H., janitor of the New College, who had died some time before: "He was a good man." Miss R.: "Grace was more manifest in his wife." Dr Duncan: "No doubt; but in some persons grace manifests itself towards God in the closet, and towards man in great conscientiousness."'

David Brown

'One day, in St Andrew Square in Edinburgh, I noticed Duncan walking with a boy – apparently an errand boy – to whom he was speaking kindly and seriously, his hand on the boy's head. And all the time the urchin, out of bravado, but with a half-frightened look, was whistling as loudly as he could. Duncan went on talking, evidently not seeing that the situation was comical.'

Henry Laurie

His Days in Glasgow

'How much he needed help and guidance in the manage-ment of his temporal affairs, will be easily understood from the recital of his eccentricities and his incurable want of punctuality. Over and over again, standing on the quay at Greenock, waiting for a steamer to take him up or down, he would go into the wrong vessel, and entering the cabin begin to read, oblivious of everything. On the steamer stopping, he would helplessly ask, "Are we at Glasgow?" (where perhaps he had to preach at a fixed hour). "Glasgow, sir! you're at Rothesay." Nothing disconcerted, he would just step into the next boat for Glasgow, and resume his studies by the way.

'He laboured in Milton Church for four years, gathering around him a small but discerning flock; occasionally startling them by his higher flights, acute sayings, and eccentric ways; suffering a severe bereavement by the death of his wife and infant child, which crushed, but mellowed his spirit; inditing verses to his first-born; pursuing his studies in an utterly irregular manner, with no set hours for anything; his books kept in such orderly disorder, that the only thing which made him angry was the attempt to dust and to replace them (on which occasions he said he "would sooner dwell in a wilderness than have his books touched"); full of mirth at times, saying to his friends at supper, "Let us see now who will tell the merriest story"; telling a friend that the one thing in the world which made him glad was, "that the glory of the Lord would endure for ever, that the Lord would rejoice in His works"; founding a class for teaching Hebrew to young ladies, and exacting as his only fee, that each person taught should teach another person Hebrew.'

William Knight

‘JUST A TALKER’

Helping at Free St Luke's

'He was most regular and exemplary in his Sabbath attendance. For twenty years he was one of our elders, took a deep interest in all our affairs, was eminently profitable in religious conference in the kirk-session, always assisted at the Communion, and frequently preached on other occasions.

'At this period of his life his great desire, was to break up the surface religion both of self-called and of sincere Christians. Some years later he entered with all his might into the awaking of the world out of death; but now his whole heart was set upon the awaking of the Church out of sleep. The "hypocrisy" of the name to live, over the stagnation and all but the corruption of death, which had been so terribly disclosed to him in Aberdeen two years after his conversion, and "the coldish admiration of Christ", which he felt creeping over him in Glasgow, he also saw prevailing in the Church. This complacent security he denounced as Antinomian; not that it rested on a doctrine verbally Antinomian, or resulted in a walk openly sinful; but it consisted with a conscience very partially alive to the holiness of God, the sinfulness of sin, and the unchangeable demands of the law, "Thou shalt love thy God with all thy heart, and thy neighbour as thyself." There was no depth or duration of doubt that he did not prefer to this carnal confidence, which he set himself most resolutely to dash in pieces; intent only to break down the pretentious evil, and leaving it to the Lord to rebuild the purified truth in the hearts and lives of his people. "A 'perhaps' of salvation," he said, "works more in some souls than all the fullness of the Gospel in others."'

A. Moody Stuart

Some Leading Aspects of Dr Duncan's Life

As a Professor

'While the direct influence of his professoriate as an academic discipline in Hebrew literature was almost nil, the spirit which breathed from the man himself and the incidental lights thrown out by him on the meaning and genius of the Hebrew economy were superlatively great. His devotional spirit touched his students and moulded many of them in ways of which they were scarcely conscious. His introductory prayer, preparatory to his lecture, sometimes protracted through a large part of the class hour, was often such a revelation of the depths of spiritual character, that it was better than the lecture which should have occupied its place; the last prayer that he ever offered with his students, in which he used the words, "Deepen our humility, enliven our zeal, and inflame our love", making a most remarkable impression on his class.

'His mode of lecturing, was more like that of the German University Professors than that which is common in Britain. With uplifted finger, he would speak, rising from his chair; and walking about his class-room in front of the benches, half communing with himself in audible soliloquy, half prelecting to his audience. Thoughts seemed borne in upon him from afar, and light after light would break upon the vision of his hearers; while his whole figure became grandly kindled by the enthusiasm of the thoughts that visited him – thoughts which almost refused to be confined within the framework of speech. Yet, when the glow of the moment died away, he would (says one who has photographed him more happily than any other) "lean back on his chair, and after taking a pinch of snuff, sum up all he had said in a happy aphoristic sentence".'

William Knight

On one occasion a student who made a shameful exhibition of ignorance of the simplest elements of Hebrew in the class received the following unexpected but scathing rebuke: "I trust, sir, for the honour of Christianity, that you will never meet with an unconverted Jew." This was as if a thunderbolt had suddenly crashed down upon the class, and made the most careless feel that their professor, with all his apparent obliviousness and patience, was not to be trifled with.'

James S. Sinclair

'I remember him coming to the class once in extreme dejection. During prayer the cloud passed away; his eye brightened, his features relaxed, and before beginning his lecture he said, "Dear young gentlemen, I have just got a glimpse of Jesus!"'

Duncan MacGregor

As a Linguist

'His knowledge of languages was so great, that Dr Guthrie spoke of him in the General Assembly as "the man who could talk his way to the wall of China"; but he knew languages better than he could use them, and he said himself that English and Latin were the only tongues in which he could speak with fluency.'

A. Moody Stuart

'"My great temptation", he said on one occasion to Miss Robertson, "is to the inordinate study of languages, as if I would learn all the languages under the sun, and fit myself to be an interpreter at the Tower of Babel."'

David Brown

'I don't know if you remember that, on the evening when you and I called at his house, we found him sitting at his dining-room table, with a single book before him. He called out, "Come away! come away! I'm just learning Bohemian by reading a translation of *Oliver Twist*. I find I get on fairly well with the aid of my knowledge of cognate languages." And there, sure enough, was a translation of *Oliver Twist* in Czech, with no dictionary or English Dickens to help him out.'

Henry Laurie

'A huge folio commonplace book now before me is curiously typical of the man – consisting of critical remarks on passages in the Hebrew and Greek Testament, with the renderings (in their originals) of the Syriac, the Vulgate, the German, Dutch, Italian, and French versions, with Rabbinical and Karaite comments; extracts from Ambrose, Gregory Nazianzen, Albert Schultens; a quantity of Hindustani and Syriac, some Arabic, Turkish, Armenian, Ethiopic, Bohemian and Spanish . . . this illustrates what he latterly mourned over, his hobby of "Linguistics" – in which he thought he had wasted much precious time, and by which he had dried up his spirit.'

David Brown

As a Preacher

A friend asked Dr John Kennedy of Dingwall on one occasion if he had ever heard Dr Duncan preach. "Yes," he replied, "on two occasions. When I was a student at Aberdeen I won a money bursary, and at the close of the session I went to Glasgow, sightseeing, and having been informed that he was preaching one week evening I went to Milton Church to hear him. The building was fairly large, but the congregation small and scattered. The light was not very good, but the brilliance of the sermon in close reasoning and soul-stirring power, I'll never forget.

"On another occasion, I was assisting Dr Begg at the Communion season in Edinburgh, and Dr Moody Stuart invited me to take the Friday evening service at Free St Luke's, which I would have done but for the closing remark in his letter, saying that otherwise he would have to fall back upon Dr Duncan. My reply was, 'Great is your privilege in having such a one to fall back upon; I'll not be coming to preach.' Then, when I estimated Dr Duncan had got under way with the service I stole quietly into the church, and heard a sermon that did not seem to have been prepared on earth, but felt as if one of the old prophets had come from within the veil to tell us what was going on there. Nothing more heavenly did I ever hear from human lips."'

James Sinclair

'In the earlier part of his course, and indeed throughout his life, his own preaching at its best was of a very high order. At its worst it was scarcely possible for him to speak without uttering weighty truths in an original and memorable form; his reading of the Bible was singularly instructive and impressive, and his prayers were the words of one standing in the immediate presence of the great Jehovah. But his preaching was too abstract, and was sometimes the slow utterance of thoughts that seemed to be gathering themselves in drops while he was in the pulpit – big drops, but with great intervals between them, and the whole occupying an excessive time before he could be satisfied that there was enough in the cup to offer a thirsting soul.'

A. Moody Stuart

His Self-Doubt and Depression

'His depression was due to various causes, some evident, others latent. "He that increaseth knowledge, increaseth sorrow", was true of him in the abundance of both; and if his knowledge had been narrower, his suffering would have been lighter. He could walk further into the sea than other men without losing his feet; but then he was tempted to wade beyond his own depth and sunk into a sea of sorrow whence he found it hard to reach the shore again . . . The seductive fruit of "the tree of knowledge" often tempted him, to the wounding of his conscience and the death of his peace. He would allow himself to be engrossed with books for days, till his heart smote him for the little time and thought given to higher objects. He said that his excessive fondness for linguistic studies caused him to forget himself, and then "God came upon him with a vengeance, and awoke him."

'In one of his forlorn states, which had lasted for weeks, he said to a friend who called on him: "I have been making idols of languages, and God is now saying to me, 'These are thy gods, and as thou hast forsaken me, I will forsake thee.'"

'Occasionally he was free from these depressions for a considerable period; but for the forty years during which I knew him he was subject to them, although they were less frequent and less severe in his latter years. Once when he had no liberty to communicate [at the Lord's Table], and had retired to the session-house, he met the beadle, an intelligent and earnest Christian, and asked him why he was not at the Table. He told him his difficulties, which Dr Duncan answered, and then in his turn he asked the Doctor why he was not there. The two had a long discussion, each severely condemning himself, and each persuading the other that he was wrong in the excessive self-condemnation, till in the end both prevailed, and both were overcome, and took their seats at the holy Supper.

'He was also in sympathy with the awakened hearers in the personal exercise of repentance and faith, and in "desiring as a new-born babe the sincere milk of the word", and sometimes he seated himself among the inquirers as one of them. He did so afterwards within two years of his death; and he did so at this time on one occasion at Kilsyth, when Mr Burns had invited inquirers to remain and to take seats set apart for themselves. Some of the assisting ministers were not prepared for this step, and did not enter into it; but to their astonishment Dr Duncan went forward to one of the separated seats. His friends, supposing that he had made a mistake, went up to him and said, "That seat is for the anxious." "But I'm anxious", was his earnest reply. He did not take his place as one out of Christ, but as anxious to know if he was certainly in Christ.

'So extreme a step was occasioned by his extreme doubting of his own salvation, yet doubt was not the only nor perhaps the chief ingredient. The only elements he had no sympathy with were pride, hardness of heart, ungodliness, worldliness. Of an orthodox minister he would sometimes say, "He's too unbroken for me."

'As regards assurance, while he doubted so much for himself, there was none more prompt or skilful in removing the doubts of others; and while he was wont to look too much within for evidences, he held most clearly the immediate shining of Christ upon the soul, and the direct witness of the Spirit.'

A. Moody Stuart

As a Christian

'Far more than other men on earth, he appeared to be at home in those many mansions in the great palace above.'

A. Moody Stuart

'What chiefly impressed many of Dr Duncan's friends both in his character and in his preaching, was the intense, ever burning, or smouldering, fire of enthusiasm for the glory of God, and the longing to realise it in his own experience. In prostrate humility he regarded himself as less than nothing and vanity: and his utmost ambition was to be a doorkeeper in the house of his God, to help forward, as an unworthy instrument, that "Kingdom" which was dearer to him than his very life.'

William Knight

'He was peculiarly alive to the danger of a semi-antinomian resting on privilege and promise, apart from the present activity of gracious affections and a daily progress in sanctification.

'An assurance of salvation founded either on the fact of conversion, or on a present faith in the Word of God, but not accompanied or followed by corresponding spiritual affections and the present exercise of grace, would have yielded no comfort to him.'

A. Moody Stuart

'Let us seek to have well-grounded marks of saintship, but when the push comes, nothing but imputed righteousness will stand the day. It was there we began, and it is there we must end, with God as a sin-forgiving God through the obedience unto the death of His only-begotten Son. And being shut up and driven back to that, will not hinder holiness but promote it, for "the grace of God that bringeth salvation hath appeared to all men, teaching us that, denying ungodliness and worldly lusts, we should live soberly, righteously, and godly in this present world".'

John Duncan

'A strict Calvinist he was, but a Catholic Christian. To use his own words, he had a strait creed for himself, but a wide one for others.'

David Brown

PART I

Shorter Sayings

ADOPTION

Adoption . . . is bestowed [on believers] in virtue of union to Christ, and is the result, not of their obedience, but of his.

AFFLICTION

The Lord is specially near to his people in affliction.

A prisoner of war is not a deserter.

The followers of the Crucified should be cross-bearers.

If we have not got a cross, alas! we may conclude that we have not got Christ, for it is the first of his gifts.

'A crown without a cross for me,' saith the natural heart. Jesus is drawing you to the cross.

To Two Sick Young Men

I trust you are led to unite the feeling of affliction with a humbling sense of sin, light affliction with heavy sin.

The Lord bless you, my dear boys. And may it please him to spare you, raise you up and send you forth with the sweet odour of sanctified affliction.

ANGELS

God upheld angels when others fell, that Christ and his Church might have servants.

The holy angels are still, and know that God is God (*Psa.* 46:10).

Michael and Gabriel know that they shall never be devils.

Who is your favourite angel? . . . Many would choose Gabriel, but the one I most desire to see is the angel who came down to strengthen my Lord in his agony in the garden.

I believe it is a mercy that our eyes are shut to save us from angel-worship.

ANTINOMIANISM

I suspect that, after all, there is only one heresy, and that is Antinomianism [that is, the sinner's quarrel with the authority of God].

What is the spirit indicated by undervaluing, or by the practical neglect of, Old Testament Scripture? It is redolent of Antinomianism. Jehovah, the great and terrible God, the holy and just, the jealous, sin-avenging God, is distasteful to the carnal mind.

They say that 'believers have nothing to do with the law.' Is there not a kingdom, and is not God a great King? and how can there be a kingdom without a law? They are God's friends, and God and they are of the same mind, but are they not his subjects?

On Coming to Christ

One kind of Antinomianism says nothing but Come; another kind refuses to say Come; the last is the worst of the two, because it lays no responsibility on the sinner.

Antinomianism as Spurious Spirituality

. . . men thinking they are so spiritual that their bodies may do as they like.

A Confession of Dr Duncan's

I fear I have been a practical Antinomian, thinking and not doing.

ARMINIANISM

Arminianism says that half of the work is God's and half is man's. Calvinism asserts that the whole is God's and the whole is man's also.

That God works half, and man the other half, is false; that God works all, and man does all, is true.

It is a monstrous doctrine: 'Christ died for me, and I may

die the second death'; only God does not hold them by their logic.

Never admit an Arminian into your pulpit.

Arminianism and Hyper-Calvinism

Hyper-Calvinism is all house and no door: Arminianism is all door and no house.

All these Englishmen, when they cease to be Arminians, see no position short of being Hyper-Calvinists.

Arminianism and Antinomianism

Intellectually, I dislike the Arminian doctrine far more than the Antinomian . . . Dr John Gill's creed is not so repugnant to my intellect as Wesley's, but Wesley comes far nearer in practice.

Gracious Arminians

Madam, you are like your own clock: it strikes the wrong hour, but the hands are always right.

To a doctor about to visit a Methodist minister: Tell him that a stout-hearted Calvinist sends him his love.

ASSURANCE OF SALVATION

Assurance is a grace, and like every other grace is sovereign.

Assurance is attainable. God does not call to what is in its own nature impossible.

We need a more forward-moving Christianity, with more of the *plerophoria pisteos* [fulness of faith] in it; which is not 'in full assurance of faith', but 'in the full sail of faith' – bearing right on with the wind; all canvas up.

Without holiness no man shall see the Lord – that principle you have to do with for evidence of your saintship, but the evidences will not do for the battle, you must go to the foundation.

Ah! confound not faith with assurance: confound not turning to God with what comes upon return to God, and comes more and more upon return to and close walking with God.

When the doctrine of assurance being necessarily contained in faith, so as to be essential to it, gets into a church, in the second generation it gets habituated to the use of the highest appropriating language by dead, carnal men.

ATHEISM

There are some minds in the Christian church who are theoretical theists but practical atheists.

It is an awful thing, that practical atheism, 'without God in the world'.

Time was when I was so sunk in atheism that once on seeing a horse I said to myself, 'There is no difference between that horse and me.'

I had a godly upbringing, but I broke off from it. I had three years of dreary atheism, and during that time I made a doctrinal atheist of a pupil of mine, who died.

I was much indebted to Dr Mearns . . . It was under him that I gave up atheism.

ATONEMENT

Ah, dear gentlemen, there is something tremendous in the atonement.

The atonement . . . the whole of Christ's obedience unto death.

The whole question of the atonement . . . must . . . be based on the two propositions, moral and legal: (i) that sin deserves punishment; and (ii) that vindictive justice belongs to God.

We are asked to throw aside every theory of the atonement and repose in the fact. But I cannot receive the atonement as a blank mystery . . . the fact of an atonement would not be clear to me apart from its reasons and relations.

The atonement is God's device through which his grace, self-moving, can flow forth, reigning through righteousness unto eternal life by Jesus Christ our Lord.

The atonement did not make God propitious, merciful, longsuffering; but God's great love said, 'I am ready to forgive, if I can do it justly', and, his infinite wisdom finding that he could do it justly in this way, he resolved on the sacrifice.

The end subserved by the atonement is the satisfaction of divine justice by the exhausting of the penalty: if it is not this, what is it?

The direct end of his atonement, indeed, is expiation of the guilt of sin; but the result of expiation is consecration and obedience.

BAPTISM

From a letter to C.H. Spurgeon: Horrible as the doctrine of baptismal regeneration is, it would be still more so if combined with those scriptural principles which are usually called Calvinism.

I can trust even for my unbaptized infant.

The water of baptism can never be wiped from the brow.

To his daughter Maria: The Lord gave you to me, and I gave you back to him before and in baptism.

To his daughter Annie: Annie, you were baptized into the name of the Father, and of the Son, and of the Holy Ghost. It is a holy name that is named upon you. Let it point you evermore to Jehovah, who sanctifieth Israel, and remind you of the call: 'be ye holy'.

I am a strong Paedo-baptist, but I favour immersion in theory; and if I built churches, I would build them for immersion. But it is an *adiaphoron* [that is, a thing indifferent].

The most awful thing for the impenitent must be to die

with the name of the Father, Son and Holy Ghost sealed upon the forehead.

BIBLE

The words of the Holy Ghost.

The Holy Scriptures are the source and storehouse of all true and saving knowledge of God.

All the communion we have with God on earth is maintained by means of the written Word.

Consider the Bible as the Word of the living God; what a majesty is in God!

The Word of the Lord is more powerful than any event in Providence.

When César Malan said to me, on an ever-to-be-remembered day, 'You have got God's Word in your mouth', I felt as if a flash of spiritual electricity had then passed through me.

The words of God are food for man, even for the Son of God as he is man.

Some one passage of Scripture, often the essence of some hundred unconnected texts, is given as a remedy to the diseased soul.

1 Peter 2:2: The 'sincere milk of the word' here cannot be understood of some portions of the Word as contradistinguished from other portions of the Word; it is the whole Word of God as milk.

1 Peter 1:23: From its own incorruptible nature, it produces an incorruptible nature; being immortal, it becomes the seed of immortal life.

God's Word, in the letter of it, is not dead. I do not read that it is dead; I read a very different thing – that 'it killeth'.

The Bible is the best school book.

Its Relation to Systematic Theology

The Bible stands in the same relation to systematic theology as nature to science, and systematic theology does for the Bible what natural science does for nature.

Its Unity

The Bible is not a congeries of books, but a unit, with organic and vital unity; not a lump, but an organism inspired by the Spirit of truth and Spirit of life.

Its Self-Authenticating Witness

The Scriptures, as a series of documents, are their own best witness-bearers.

The evidence for Scripture is Scripture.

Its Imperishable Nature

The words of men are perishable, being the words of perishable men; but . . . his [that is, God's] words resemble himself – they are imperishable, immortal.

Its Leading Themes

God, a Spirit, holy, just and good; God's law, spiritual, holy, just and good; sin against God, exceeding sinful; salvation from sin, and that of God – these are the main themes of Scripture.

Its Interpretation

Coming to Scripture with ready-made canons of interpretation looks more like an attempt to induce, than to educe, the meaning.

The correct exposition of Holy Scripture is that on which the whole building of solid theological learning must be based.

If asked what I consider the qualifications for a good expositor of Holy Writ, I would answer these three: (1) a heart seasoned with grace; (2) a head filled with good common sense; (3) a mind stored with all that liberal education which aids exposition in general, and that of these holy books in particular.

We are not at liberty to leave apostolic exegesis for our own ideas.

There is a true doctrine of development in the Scriptures.

Its Relation to the Work of the Spirit

The character of God's inspired Word and the work of God's Spirit in the souls of renewed men are in perfect unison. 'Every word of God is pure.' 'The fear of the Lord is clean.'

Its Relation to Christ

It's Christ in the Bible that makes the Bible a glorious Bible.

The supreme excellency of these Scriptures is that they testify of Christ.

Oh, what a blessing to think that the unfolding as well as the inspiration of Scripture is by Christ.

It's a shut book to you; it's an open book to him.

Oh, it were well for us when we read Scripture to think of the eye of Christ and our eyes meeting on the Scripture.

The Old Testament

To surrender the Old Testament is to surrender also the New.

The commencement of the sacred volume sweeps away at once all systems of false religion, and introduces the self-existent Creator.

The New Testament

What is our New Testament system but Hebrew thought in a Greek clothing?

Were I a younger man, and to begin my studies again, the

four gospels would bulk more prominently in my attention than they have done.

John was an intense intuitionalist. His gospel and first epistle, taken together, make a good apologetical manual. His epistle gives the philosophy of the gospel.

For the balancing of truth, there is nothing like the Pauline letters; for vitality and freshness, there is nothing like the facts of the gospel.

Its Inspiration

God employs human speech; but he himself selects the words that are to express his thoughts.

Biblical writers: True, they were the pen-men of the Holy Spirit, but then they were pen-men.

It is a grand evidence for the inspiration of the apostles that the theology of the post-apostolic Fathers is so puerile.

Its Authority

We are bound to believe on the authority of God, whenever we have reason to believe that God has really spoken.

God speaks. He speaks in his Word to all to whom it comes.

I know not what standard we are to go on, if Scripture is not the Word of God.

Shorter Sayings

Its Language

The poetry of the sublime rises to its very highest level in Scripture, because we have the sublimity of form added to the sublimity of the theme.

The Hebrew language is peculiarly rich in religious-moral terms, though scanty enough in others. The reason is evident – it chronicled a revelation.

The Greek mind was abstract, the Hebrew concrete.

Not only the best things are in the Bible, but they are said in the best way.

The Spirit of God is not guilty of tautology.

Translations

Oh, it is a pitiable thing for a poor silly puppy of a sciolist to stand up in the pulpit vexing the people by shaking their confidence in our good English translation.

The three best translations of the Bible, in my opinion, are, in order of merit, the English, the Dutch and Diodati's Italian version.

Exhortations Regarding Scripture

Believe not any man on his own mere word. Sacredly reserve your faith for the Word of the living God.

Search, scrutinize, ransack the Scriptures.

Keep close to the Bible. Pray for the teaching of the Holy Spirit, and subordinately to this, study the works, expository and symbolical, of the great Reformers.

We think of self-application instead of Christ-application . . . It is man's duty to study the Word prayerfully. To purge by it is God's work.

Its Abuse

The Jews were bibliolatrous in thinking that eternal life was in the Scriptures. They testify it, but have it not.

Those who think they are the children of God when they are not, take to themselves those portions of the divine truth which have no immediate bearing upon them, and so prevent the coming home to them of those that have.

Dr Duncan's Own Attitude to Scripture

We would not shun the truth, the most searching and most dreadful of the truths of God.

Oh, how precious is the Holy Scripture!

God's words are law to me now, and I am a child at his feet, seeking simply to learn of him.

BIBLE CHARACTERS

If Adamic blood flows in all our veins, Abrahamic blood flows spiritually in every Christian's veins.

Cain was a deist; that is, an impenitent theist.

In Noah we have the first account of justification by grace.

Asaph is a less-severely tried Job, and a better instructed, being an Israelite, while Job was only a Shemite – Terahite or Nahorite.

Isaiah I take to be the most Pauline of the Old Testament men; Ezekiel the most Petrine.

The prophets prophesied by the Spirit of Christ – the apostles preached by the commission of Christ.

The widow (Luke 21:2): We can almost think she cast in those two mites into the treasury with a sigh that the offering was so small.

John . . . with the eagle eye, is content to gaze, and to rest gazing, on the life which is the light of men.

Apollos (aner logicos, Acts 18:24): Not [an] eloquent, but an intellectual man, a ratiocinative thinker.

Moses

Diverse as they are in many respects, I know no man more Johannean than Moses. His meekness is closely allied to Johannean love.

I have often pitied Moses, for he had a stiff rebellious race to manage.

His faith reposed in God not only for what God would do for him, but for what God would graciously . . . fit him to do.

Paul

I look on the apostle Paul as the greatest genius that ever lived.

Two things strike me in that wonderful sermon of Paul at Athens: his considerable tact in recognizing all the good he found in Athens, and how he laid the axe to the root of the tree of Attic pride.

Paul was from first to last a man of law, and the Pauline revelations of law and gospel have taken a very deep hold on me.

Paul, whose principal aim as a writer seems to be to unfold the whole unity of the divine plan.

I bless God for Paul.

Look at the zeal of the apostle Paul – the edge which he received has never a day blunted.

It is the characteristic of the apostle Paul that, whatever be the subject of which he treats, he always finds his way easily to the cross, to Christ crucified.

'I belong to Paul.' No you don't . . . Paul belongs to you (*1 Cor.* 3:22).

Paul – the little rickety man of the big strong fist (*Gal.* 6:11).

Scribes and Pharisees

. . . the austere sanctimoniousness of the Scribes and Pharisees.

. . . the antinomianism, Arminianism and hypocrisy of the Pharisees.

On hearing a pharisaic woman suspicious of a prodigal's conversion: What! Has the elder brother come back again? The scoundrel!

BOOKS

Dr Duncan's Idols

These are my 'world'. What social dissipation is to another man, study is to me – worldliness.

Recommendations

I urge the formation of synodal libraries throughout Scotland. Manse libraries (a permanent part of the manse property) are good; but synodal libraries should be instituted, and they should contain the rarer folios.

Biographies

There are three biographies of which I never tire: Augustine's, Bunyan's and Halyburton's. The first is by far the deepest, the second the richest and the most genial, and with Halyburton I feel great intellectual congruity.

BRETHRENISM

The Plymouth Brethren assert there should be no sects, because there is no visible church; nevertheless, they add one.

Romish Puseyism is the carcase of Christianity: Ultra-Evangelicalism, which runs to seed in Plymouthism, is the ghost of Christianity.

CALVINISM

There is no such thing as Calvinism. The teachings of Augustine, Remigius, Anselm and Luther were just pieced together by one remarkable man, and the result baptized with his name.

There is no such thing as Calvinism. It is Augustinianism and Anselmism, with Luther's development taken in.

The late eminent Mr Bain, minister of the Gaelic Chapel, Greenock, was once told of some young licentiate, that he had 'mastered Calvinism': 'I wish [said Dr Duncan] that you could rather tell me that Calvinism had mastered him.'

On Grace

The Calvinist affirms a grace of God towards his own children which the Arminian denies towards any creature; so that Calvinism is an intensive exhibition of divine grace, while Arminianism presents us with an extensive and diffusive one.

Misunderstood

Calvinism, as I have heard Lutherans define it . . . is so horrible a thing that I shrink aghast at the thought of it!

Calvinism, Pelagianism and Arminianism

Every unrenewed Arminian is a Pelagian, and every unrenewed Calvinist is a fatalist.

Calvinism and Pelagianism are the only consistent systems. Arminianism is utterly inconsistent and irrational.

Its Height

I think I'm a high Calvinist. I have no objection to the height of the Calvinists, but I have objections to the miserable narrowness of some, the miserable narrowness.

As Calvinism rises to the infinite, it can't be too high.

Calvinism and the Free Offer

God has taught me that what they call Calvinism is God's way of grace and salvation – that is, evangelical Calvinism, with the free offer of the gospel. Did I make a free offer of the gospel in my preaching? Did I not clog it with legal enactments?

On the Decrees

I have never entered the door of either supra- or infra-lapsarian Calvinism.

CHRIST

His Divine Sonship

It is a begotten Sonship; not at the incarnation, for then God became man, man did not become God; not at the resurrection, for then he was declared, not constituted Son of God with power. It is not one act or work, but eternal, timeless.

Eternal generation is neither an act nor a progressive work, but like eternity itself, it must be timeless.

He is the eternal life by the eternal generation.

Angels and archangels forever prostrate themselves before him, as the eternal, co-equal Son of the Father.

The Son of Man is the Son of God.

His Person as Mediator

In Christ there is a full exhibition of God.

Human excellency in its perfection united to eternal Godhead.

All the intercourse which God has had with man has been through Jesus Christ.

There is nothing but Christ between us and hell; and, thanks be to God, we need nothing else.

Christ is a wonderful Being; we could never do without Christ.

Christ is a needed, a suitable, an accessible Saviour.

Adam was holy man, and Christ is holy man; but Adam was mere man, and Christ is God-man.

If I think I am not among the lost, Christ is no Saviour for me. But whether we believe it or not, our souls are lost.

The Messiah is *Theanthropos* – Emmanuel, God with us; and the doctrine of the *Theanthropos* is the keystone of the theology and anthropology of the Old Testament.

Christ is a study.

The Person of Christ is not sufficiently studied or contemplated by the majority of modern theologians.

Jesus Christ, being the cornerstone, unites the prophets to the apostles.

Christ is glorious: life is sweet.

Consider Jesus Christ, and if you can't consider Christ, consider the lilies of the field, how they grow.

The Lord has not revealed the names of the elect saved, but he has revealed the name of the elect Saviour.

Christ either deceived mankind by conscious fraud, or he was himself deluded and self-deceived, or he was divine. There is no getting out of this trilemma. It is inexorable.

His Incarnation

The form of God – the form of a servant! (*Phil.* 2:6–7). What a stoop that was!

In the incarnation, Christ took our flesh, that he might give us his Spirit.

To believe in the incarnation is to be a Christian.

We make far too little of the incarnation; the Fathers knew much more of the incarnate God. Some of them were oftener at Bethlehem than at Calvary . . . We are not too often at the cross, but we are too seldom at the cradle.

It is true that scarcely any of us in Scotland give due prominence to the incarnation.

His Human Nature and Character

In Jesus is all human beauty.

Jesus Christ . . . is the perfection of humanity, its ideal made real.

Can you conceive anything more beautiful than the character of Jesus Christ?

Jesus is lovely.

He was holy, harmless, undefiled and separate from sinners, but the publicans and sinners felt in him an attraction.

In him we behold a beauty of sinless humanity.

In Jesus we behold . . . all the beauty of perfect humanity.

He is sweet, but sin is bitter.

Christ is more a giver than a receiver.

His Life on Earth

'He became obedient unto death' (*Phil.* 2:8). It was not a passing from disobedience to obedience, but a passing from a lower state and course of obedience into a higher task of obedience.

His obedience unto death is that by which we are redeemed; that . . . by which the many are justified . . . that to which God has predestined his people to be conformed.

Ignorance cannot be attributed to Christ at any time, though nescience may; for that is simple non-knowledge, not ignorance of something that ought to be known.

Christ's study was his Father's law.

Man thought to rise above law. God, the Lawgiver, comes down and honours the law by coming under it. Christ is at once the eternal Lawgiver and the Subject of the law and the Perfect Exhibition of it.

Almost without exception the whole teaching of the Lord Jesus Christ was founded on Old Testament declarations.

His Death

Among all deaths there is no death like one death; there are the deaths of sinners; this one death is the death of the Lord of glory.

Isaiah 53:5: Was ever the like heard of? Will ever the like be heard of again? It is the wonder of the universe.

Christ crucified is the centre of Christology.

Divine vengeance found sin in us, but Christ was made sin for us.

Do not sins deserve death? And so Christ once endured the death which sins deserve.

The Father was willing that the iniquity should be charged on him, though not as the doer of it, yet as the answerer for it.

Our Lord was always without sin in him, but he had a great load of sin on him.

Christ died for us, and by dying for us obtained right in us.

Justice required satisfaction, but love gave vicarious satisfaction.

The soul of the Messiah was given for me, a sinner; death to him and life to me.

The eternal punishment endured by the sinner can never be finished, as the infinite punishment endured by Christ was; it will ever fall short of legal acquittal.

Take away the substitution, and all that remains for me is this: 'Jesus tried to make us good; but, good man, he failed.'

He was to drink the cup of curse and condemnation . . . He did not leave one bitter drop for us, but drank it to the dregs; and instead, he put into our hands the cup of salvation.

Christ got that cup of wrath which was ours.

Ay, ay, d'ye know what it was – dying on the cross, forsaken by his Father? D'ye know what it was? What? What? It was damnation, and damnation taken lovingly . . . It was damnation, and he took it lovingly.

You remember one of my favourite tracts, 'The Poor Negress'. The broken English leaves out the connections, and brings in the big facts. 'He die, or we die: He die, we no die.'

Sacrifice is founded on the connection that is between sin and death.

The death could not be inflicted unless the sin was imputed. So, the nature of a sacrifice is the death of the innocent for the guilty, by the transference of the guilt to the innocent.

Nothing but the death of Christ could put away sin.

The offering of the sacrifice is perfected, but the application is not completed.

Remember that though it was not the eternal Godhead that suffered, but the humanity, it was a person and not a nature that suffered – God-man.

It seems to me a terrible thing to say that there was no intrinsic necessity for Christ's death, for then we virtually say that he died for sin that he need not have died for.

Death had an apparent, Jesus had the real victory.

He is the Victor. He does not say, 'Who enables us to gain the victory', but, 'Who giveth us the victory.' The victory is Christ's death.

The blood of Christ . . . having met the demands of justice in God . . . meets the demands of justice in the awakened conscience.

To die for the sake of sinners whose sin is not actually taken away would be a clear waste of moral action.

The blood of Jesus Christ is surely a ransom for ten thousand pits!

Christ, by bearing sin . . . bears sin away.

I have been at the point of death, the point of death. But I found that the one great mysterious death of Calvary was all I needed at the point of death.

Jesus died . . . believers sleep.

In reply to the question: 'Is there any news today?': Oh, yes, this is always news: 'The blood of Jesus Christ cleanseth us from all sin.'

The expulsion from Eden was an awful thing; the deluge was an awful thing; the destruction of Sodom and Gomorrah was an awful thing; the events of the last day will be awful; hell is very awful. There is something more awful still – it is the cross of the Lord Jesus.

Oh, look to his death for life – for life that leads to everlasting life at the end of this earthly life.

His Burial

The body of Christ was not separated from the God-head. The soul of Christ was not separated from the Godhead.

His Death and Resurrection

He must die, for he could not purchase otherwise. He must rise, for he could not otherwise exercise his Lordship over his purchase.

He had power to lay down his life to procure, and he had power to take it again to bestow salvation.

I am inclined to draw the inference, since Jesus died and rose again, I may be in heaven yet.

His Resurrection

We have in a risen Saviour the proofs of a power beyond the most dreaded of all hostile powers – the power of death.

As sure as Christ is risen, we are not in our sins.

His Kingly Session

The Dust of the Earth is on the throne of the Majesty on High.

There was a load of sin on him, but there is now a crown of glory on his head.

Christ is God's (*1 Cor.* 3:23). God's Christ, God's Servant, God's Prophet, God's Priest, God's King.

How precious is that part of Christ's kingly office, 'subduing us to himself'! I find it as essential to my salvation as the atonement.

A brother's heart beats upon the throne. He who now sits on the throne of the universe was once a helpless infant on his mother's breast.

His Second Coming

When Christ, who is our life, shall appear, then shall ye also appear with him in glory . . . What a head! and what members!

He quickens the dead soul, and will quicken the mortal body.

Come, Lord Jesus. All things are disjointed, but thou bearest up the pillars.

Till he comes it is the reign of hope; when he comes it is the reign of grateful remembrance.

His Lordship Over Us

We are not the world's, not Satan's, not our own; we are the Lord's.

Our Redeemer, our glorious Emmanuel, is the Lord of angels.

He is the universal disposer of man's state . . . here . . . at death, and throughout eternity.

Jesus knows all events, manages all events.

What is it to call Jesus Lord? It is to worship him.

The Centre of Heaven

Christ is the centre of all. Placed on him, the eyes of Abel, of Abraham, Isaac and Jacob meet the eyes of the last of the saints of God upon earth.

Around the One, who died once, shall be found the many . . . who ought to have died eternally.

Christ and History

The lines of history meet in the history of Christ. Blessed is the man whose individual history falls in and under the history of Christ; if not, he is swept away with the burning.

The Living One

Jesus is the Living One. He hath life in himself underived. He is the well-spring of all derived life. Life is natural, essentially natural to him. Even in death he lived.

Life to the lost, to the dead, could come from no other source than the eternal life itself.

His Love for Sinners

We could not prepay such love, and we cannot repay such love.

The children of men have despised and rejected him, but we never read that he despised and rejected men.

Three stages in expressing his love: First, giving himself;

then, purifying; then, presenting to himself. He gave himself that he might purify, and he purifies that he may present.

Some have heard Christ say, 'Ye are of your father the devil', who have heard him say afterwards, 'I go to my Father and your Father.'

Imputation

We, by nature, are foolish; Christ is made unto us wisdom. We are unrighteous; he is made unto us righteousness. We are unholy; he is made unto us sanctification. We are lost; he is made unto us redemption.

He is wisdom to foolish me – he is righteousness to guilty me – he is sanctification to unholy me – he is redemption to ruined me.

He is all that is excellent, but I am all that is vile.

Christ's righteousness is God's present to men . . . When it falls on an oppressed conscience it is an astonishing joy.

Let us seek to have well-grounded marks of saintship, but when the push comes, nothing but imputed righteousness will stand the day. It was there we began, and it is there we must end.

Our Sanctifier

He who gave himself as the redemption-price must be himself the purifier of his own bride.

The buying time is past; the presenting time is future; the purging time is now.

No life of faith on the Son of God but for the life of the Son in me (*Gal.* 2:20).

Regarding Christ and his Bride: If he is careful to purify, she surely should be careful to be purified.

A Summary of His Work

Christ has a three-fold work: a work for us, a work in us, and a work by us.

His Presence in His Church

Jesus is present – present in his church, as he is not in the world. As eternal God, he filleth immensity with his presence; but as Mediator . . . he is peculiarly, mystically, but really with his church.

Coming to Christ

It will not do to tell a man that he may come to Christ, but that he must come, and that he cannot come; that he must come, or he will look to another to come for him, and that he cannot come, or he will look to himself for salvation.

We bring . . . not only our sins, but our sinfulness to Christ.

Christ casts out none that come to him, but he searches all that come.

We come with the guilt of our sin to Christ, who died for our sins, the just for the unjust; and we come with our sinful nature to Christ, that our old man may be crucified, and that by the Spirit of life in Christ Jesus there may be found the new man.

You don't make Christ a present when you give him your heart; you only give him that which he has already bought.

Come to him, come again, come closer.

Be sure of coming to Christ: be sure of abiding in Christ: be sure of bringing forth fruit to Christ.

Receiving Christ

By God's grace we do not give ourselves to Christ and receive him; but receive him and give ourselves to him. Ay, something goes even before that: he apprehends us, whereupon we follow on.

We must first give ourselves to Christ before he will accept anything else from us . . . But something goes before that: we must first receive him.

If you receive Christ for anything, you receive him for everything.

How shall we, in a weak and little heart, hold the glory of Christ, and support the weight of glory? By being strengthened with all might by the Spirit in the inner man – so, only so.

On the Galatian heresy: Circumcision or Christ – not circumcision and Christ.

To an hospitable unbeliever: It grieves me to the heart to think that you can be so kind to the servant and keep the Master standing at the door.

Looking to Christ

Let the blind try; let them look.

If ye be blind, and cannot see, let your blind eyeballs be towards him.

We are sure that the eye that sees him once would never cease to gaze on him.

'Behold the Lamb of God.' It is a sight well deserving that we should turn aside and behold, that our eyes should be turned away from everything in the universe just to look to Christ.

It is our duty to fix the eyes on the Lamb of God, blind or not blind.

The eyes of the Old Testament church and the eyes of the New Testament church meet on Christ.

Oh, behold him! Behold his Person, grace, work, heart! Oh, there is none like Christ! None like Christ!

I have been for a moment looking out to Jesus, who is, and was, and is to come; who liveth, and was dead.

I would see Jesus. I am thinking on his name distantly, but I would see him.

Knowing Christ

Though the knowledge of Christ is composed of parts, the parts are not knowable as parts. There is a whole in the knowledge of Christ, to which the world cannot attain.

Oh! it is miserably little that I know of Jesus Christ – miserably little.

Oh, that I had better learned to count all things but loss for the excellency of the knowledge of Christ Jesus, my Lord!

To his students after prayer in his Hebrew class: Dear young gentlemen, I have just got a glimpse of Jesus.

As long as I am thinking of Christ I'm happy.

Let us contemplate Christ.

The contemplation of Christ is full of blessedness to the soul.

Beholding the Lamb of God, we become lamb-like.

Worshipping Christ

The worship of Christ, if he be not God, is idolatry, and the Christian religion damnable sin. So we must be very sure that Christ is God before we worship him.

Loving Christ

Loving Jesus . . . It is the comprehension of desirable beauty.

To a Free Church of Scotland elder who sent him a gift: I

trust that . . . the real motive is love to One higher far than any portion of the church or even the whole church, even him 'who loved the church and gave himself for it.'

To an appreciative congregation: I know you love me, but I did not die for you.

On the woman with the ointment: If thy conscience will not have the forgiveness . . . then Christ cannot have the great love.

The Attraction or Attractiveness of Christ

Christ is all attraction . . . The world thinks him . . . all repulsion, but he is all attraction.

He is all attraction, but lifted up on the cross he is most of all attractive. All his drawing power is concentrated there.

Woe . . . for the man who has not experience of more drawing than he is able to give an account of in words.

There is an unknown attractiveness in Jesus Christ.

The Necessity of Possessing Christ

Those that can part with Christ are no Christians.

It is death to be separated from Christ for a moment.

If we are not Christ's, whose are we? Our own.

His All-Sufficiency

We are made up of wants – of wants as creatures, and deeper wants as sinners – but for all our wants there is in him all riches.

It is on his bounty you are to live, who is not only a bountiful Giver, but a bountiful Giver of a very peculiar kind – a bountiful Husband.

His All-Suitableness

Jesus is a suitable Saviour to a lost sinner.

I came to see that God had a Covenant of Grace, and that this Covenant embraced a salvation that is suited to my *case*, but said nothing about my *person*. From that I came to the Mediator of the Covenant, and the Person and Offices of Christ, and I saw a Saviour suited to me.

His Preciousness as Our Hope

Precious Jesus! Precious Jesus! Words cannot tell the value, power and blessedness of a believer's hope in him!

Christ Inseparable from His Benefits

As soon may a man bottle up daylight as have a gospel of benefits without the immediate shining of the Sun of Righteousness.

I would not preach the benefits of redemption without preaching Christ, but neither would I preach a benefitless Christ.

CHRISTIANITY

It is a great historical fact; if we reject it we must explain it to vindicate the rejection; we must find its source in natural causes, and this you cannot do.

Christianity does not tell me all I would like to know . . . but while it enlightens my reason as to my duties, it gives me sufficient light as to the ultimate mysteries, to prevent their paralysing me altogether.

Our Christianity is not primitive Christianity.

On Reading the Children's Missionary Record: I like to learn Christianity like a little bairn.

A Warning about Selfish Christianity

It may assume the form of deepest experimentalism, but it is the experience of a heart whose feelings are knit and contracted and withering in itself.

CHURCH

The pulse of the Christian church beats from its heart in heaven.

There is no salvation but in the church, and no glory given to God but in the church.

What comes through Christ is the church; for it is through Christ, by the Spirit of Christ, to the members of Christ.

He loved her! And why? I cannot tell: she cannot tell: angels cannot tell: he knows himself.

On earth he came, he that is from above, to meet with her that is from beneath, to purchase and to betroth her.

Those who love the Lamb must love the Bride, the Lamb's wife. They have no true love to the Lamb who have no true love to the Bride, the Lamb's wife . . . this poor, puny, selfish Christianity is no Christianity at all.

To cleave to the Lamb – that's the heart of the Bride.

Oh, when the eye has seen the Lamb, it has seen the best sight; but next to that is the sight of the Bride, the Lamb's wife.

I would like to see the Lamb; I would like to see the Father of the Lamb; I would like to see the Spirit of the Lamb; but next to that I would like to see the Lamb's Wife. I would like to see her; I would like to be her.

Its Unity and Fellowship

Seas and continents separate in space, but the church of Christ is one in him.

The present principle that is to unite the church in the possession of the one faith is love . . . Love is the great inward uniting principle.

It is a beautiful thing to see an assured and strong believer tender to weak faith, and a weak believer thanking God for his grace to the strong. It is a beautiful sight to look on Mr Greatheart guiding Mr Fearing.

We forget the best part of the church when we forget the church triumphant.

It would be well for Christendom if all the members of Christ's catholic church would endeavour to preserve the unity of the Spirit, and think oftener of the many and major points in which they agree than the few and minor ones in which they differ.

When we all reach yonder country, we shall wonder what foolish bairns we have been.

What community of sorrow or of joy have you with the body, and with each individual member?

The world is crying out for a working church and a united working church – truthing it in love.

A Warning

We . . . have cause to fear, not that the kingdom of God should become extinct, but lest it should be taken from us, and given to a nation that would bring forth the fruits of it.

An Encouragement

[The Lord Jesus Christ] will not suffer Satan, or all the power of hell, to extinguish a candle which is answering its purpose, and giving light to those around.

Early Church Worship

Before that [the coming of heresies] the disciples came together, and read, and prayed, and exhorted one another. Their words were hortatory, not doctrinal. They read the Scriptures, and said, 'Let's be Christians!', and partook of the sacrament, and sang, and went home.

Church Discipline

No man can be deposed from the church catholic for doctrinal heresy. He may be suspended from this or that individual church, but not cut off from the universal church of Christ.

You cannot deal judicially with a man for a logical blunder, though you may deem him intellectually weak or confused.

Church and State

Voluntaryism: The Voluntary principle is not only anti-Christian, but atheistical.

In Relation to the Jewish Theocracy

I do not see that the Christian church is now under the theocratic law of the Jews . . . It will not do to bring us under bondage to any purely Jewish practice.

CHURCH GOVERNMENT

Was not the primitive church government parochial episcopacy?

In the theocracy of the Jews we have the germ of a despotism under the law of liberty. But it was too perfect for corrupt humanity, and the polity of the New

Testament is better than it, though the spirit of theocracy cannot die.

THE CHURCH IN SCOTLAND

That is a fine saying of Sack of Bonn in his history of the Scottish Church: 'In Scotland there are no sects, only parties.' That is a fine testimony from a foreigner.

The Free Church is dearer to me than myself.

I rejoice in being a member of a Free Church, but I rejoice still more in being a member of the catholic church of the Lord Jesus.

Dr Duncan's Priorities

I'm first a Christian, next a Catholic, then a Calvinist, fourth a Paedo-baptist, and fifth a Presbyterian. I cannot reverse this order.

CIVIL GOVERNMENT AND RULERS

A despotism would be the very perfection of government, if we could get so good a sovereign always that his simple will might be absolute law. But this is impossible, and the next best thing is what we have in England – limited constitutional monarchy.

Bishops in the House of Lords

As lords they are not spiritual, and as spiritual they are not lords.

Dr Duncan's Prayers for the Government

O Lord, bless our sinful, godless, Sabbath-breaking Privy Council. Thou knowest that thou art not honoured there, for they profane thy holy day by their meetings for state business.

O Lord, bless the high courts of parliament now assembled. Thou knowest that thou art not honoured there, where potsherd warreth with potsherd. Do thou be there to over-rule their deliberations.

COMFORT

To a congregation bereaved of its minister: Dear brethren, I can weep with you, but cannot console you: that work is reserved for the other Comforter.

Suspect that comfort which does not maintain and tend at least to deepen conviction.

CONSCIENCE

Whilst God imputes sin, conscience . . . likewise imputes sin.

What conscience demands is just what the law demands.

. . . responsibility – the primary truth of conscience.

Since my own conscience tells me that I have done the sin, and declares that I should die the death, nothing else can satisfy that conscience till the deserved death come.

Conscience is the great root of theism, and it leads within the veil . . . God must be distinct from the cosmos, or conscience is all a lie.

So far as conscience is ethical, it is a manifestation of God's nature in men; so far as it is law, it is a manifestation of his will.

There is a wonderful power in a good conscience.

Where there is no conscience there can be nothing penal.

Conscience is not produced by me, and it testifies to another beyond me. Conscience is the voice of a lawgiver.

I think we get out of ourselves, to a rock higher than we are, if we follow conscience to its source.

If we lose conscience, we lose dignity; we become pulses, not men.

I affirm that conscience testifies to law, to moral law . . . not in the secular sense . . . nor in the sectarian sense . . . but in the primitive moral sense in which the lawyers use it, as the expression of an authoritative will.

I can scarcely think that a man will perish who has a tender conscience.

I hurt my conscience yesterday by reading an erroneous book, and I have not got myself right again.

It's an evil conscience that clamours down the gospel of God's grace.

If my conscience turn a rebel against my God, I must believe my God rather than my conscience.

Conscience in Fallen Man

Conscience is out of order through the Fall.

That sin deserves to be punished is a truth of conscience. Heathen men know 'that they who do such things are worthy of death' (*Rom.* 1:32).

The voice of conscience is very feeble in fallen men, and the voice of depravity very loud and imperious, and it silences it.

Conscience and Atonement

Conscience quickened by contact with the divine Word demands a satisfaction which man has not rendered and is unable to render.

God announces to conscience the principles upon which it can rest. Can God be just, and pardon me?

Does God pardon as a mere sovereign? . . . Conscience asserts that a gratuitous pardon would not be just . . . It cries out for restitution of some sort, and expiation of some sort.

If we have conscience of sin, this is our first duty: to bring conscience of sin to the blood of Christ and leave it there – ever to carry about with us a conscience which speaks of offended satisfied justice, a provoked reconciled God.

Conscience has a right to speak about the evil of sin, but conscience has not a right to refuse the blood which God accepts.

How little are our consciences permeated by the blood of Christ!

Conscience and Justification

The healthy conscience . . . repudiates justification divorced from sanctification. A justification that left us as it found us, conscience would disown.

A Dead Conscience

I have more than once seen the calmness of the brutish ignorance of an unawakened conscience on the very verge of eternity. It was an awful calmness.

Conscience in Children

If you address the children, you will find that what lays hold of them is everything that appeals to the conscience.

CONTROVERSY

Controversialists should always begin by concession. It is courteous, and therefore conciliates.

Age rubs down a good deal the controversial spirit in a man.

The mere controversialist, who would always be in the thick of the fight with error, is no more worthy of respect than the pugilist.

The controversial minds are like the lean cattle of Egypt; they are very greedy, and are none the fatter for their feeding.

The great controversy that is coming is about the existence of God.

CONVERSION

Dr Duncan was overheard thus addressing a beggar woman on the garden side of Moray Place, Edinburgh, 'Now, you'll promise me that you'll seek. And mind, seeking will not save you; but it is your duty; and if you seek you'll find, and finding will save you.'

Sinners need conversion.

You must be converted or you cannot go to heaven.

Why do you need conversion? Because you are in the wrong road . . . you are in the road the termination of which is hell.

As the conversion of the least sinner is very difficult . . . the conversion of the greatest sinner is possible.

The conversion of sinners is a matter in which the gracious God takes the deepest interest.

O sinner, lay it to heart: thy conversion, perhaps, concerns thee little; thy conversion concerns thy God very much.

Observe: conversion, as wrought by the Spirit of God, is God's act; conversion, as wrought within a sinner, denotes his acting also.

Beware of resting short of giving the whole heart unto God. Conversion is a great work of God, and of man under the mighty power of the Holy Ghost; a divine work upon a rational being having an understanding, will, and affections. Hence 'Turn ye, turn ye', and also the souls' cry, 'Turn us and we shall be turned.' Yea, that very command, 'Make you a new heart' must be obeyed. 'Ye have purified your hearts, keep yourselves in the love of God', all these things must be done. Make not slim work of conversion.

By Divine Power

While nothing is required of a sinner but just simply to come back [that is, to God], power is needed for the bringing of the sinner back.

When moral suasion only is employed, men remain dead; when the soul is quickened, the Word is felt to be quick and powerful.

To his daughter: Oh, my dear Annie, I cannot make you a Christian, but Christ can.

When God is away, the sinner is concealed among the crowd . . . When God catches him, he individualises him.

Its Diversity

God does not lead us all by the same way.

Some he draws gently into the kingdom; others it is impossible to pull up. They never come to their senses till they strike their heads against one of his eternal laws, and get them well battered.

There is a honeymoon in this as well as in the earthly marriage, but do not expect the fatted calf to be killed every day.

Warnings

The man who would rest content with God's mercy at some future time, is the man who is content to rest without it.

When men come to adopt a stereotyped manner of recognizing God, or of conversion to him, you may be sure there is some human conceit in it.

There are some modern theologians who seem to exclude God from the work of conversion.

Its Humbling Effect on Us

How humbling to man to be brought into the presence of his God a convicted, condemned, hell-deserving sinner! And when salvation is offered him, and he accepts it, it is a gey doon-come [considerable comedown] to be told that neither his repentance nor his faith is his own!

Desire for the Conversion of Sinners

It is the characteristic of the people of God that they desire the conversion of sinners unto God; they are not . . . in a healthy state where this desire is not active.

CONVICTION OF SIN

If you have conviction enough to bring you to Christ, however little it may be, it is quite enough.

Convictions are not needed to make us welcome to Christ, but to make him welcome to us.

Convictions are not lost by our coming to Christ. The deepest convictions . . . are obtained after coming.

With regard to convictions, do not stifle them, do not bury them amidst employments, amusements or vain hopes; seek them, cherish them.

You may have some conviction of sin without returning to God.

When the Holy Spirit sows convictions, Satan seeks . . . to mingle unbelief, doubts and discouragements.

In many cases the agony of convictions, and their protraction, come not simply from the depth of conviction, but from unbelief of the gospel and a proud unwillingness to be saved by grace.

CREATION

God created the universe for his glory and the manifestation of his attributes.

We cannot conceive creation.

If I reach the fact of creation I reach the infinite, for the infinite power alone is creative.

I see no refuge from Pantheism except in a doctrine of creation *ex nihilo*.

Creation came before the Fall; we were God's before we were the devil's.

God filled the world with man: sin filled the world with sinners.

Creation and Evolution

Sin and holiness are antithetic, and you cannot connect them by tracing back to a common fountain-head. Therefore, I say, the universe has not been evolved.

I admit that evolution is not atheistic, but I deny that there is any scientific evidence for it. And I think we should have something better than a guess or a conjecture in a matter so weighty.

I wonder how, if men lived a million of years, they should have no history before 5,000 years.

Where is your half-formed geologic man? . . . Why have we no fossil link? There is no existing species which shade into each other by insensible degrees. And development could not have gone on as by leaps.

CREATURES

Dogs have a kind of reason; instinct is just a word for our ignorance. Man is their god, their highest idea of being.

There are times when . . . I cannot read my Bible and I

cannot pray. But I go into my garden to consider the lilies how they grow.

All existence is being out of or from God.

CREEDS AND CONFESSIONS OF FAITH

The creeds are to me next in value to the Scriptures. Undoubtedly, of all human compositions, they are most precious.

This is a time which demands all the friends of Bible truth to rally around that divine standard, and I fear much that any change made at present on symbolical books would rather deteriorate than improve.

Doctrines, whether of individual teachers or of a church, embodied in her symbolical books [Catechisms and Confessions of Faith] can have no authority but what they derive from the volume of inspiration.

I have always wondered that the Augsburg Confession contains so full a doctrine about grace, and stops short of conclusions which to me seem necessary.

I am ashamed to confess that once I declared my belief in the [Westminster] Confession of Faith when I scarcely believed any part of it. This day I have, with my whole heart and with a full faith, declared my belief in it all.

DEATH

Death is the severance of things which were once united, and which were meant to remain united.

God is the life of the soul, as the soul is the life of the body; and death spiritual severs the first connection, as death physical cuts the second.

Death is the great divider.

Death is not a positive thing. It is the absence of life.

Death is a separator; he separates soul and body, and he separated for a time the soul and body of our Lord . . . but he could separate neither the soul nor the body from the divinity.

Death's work is to separate, to separate entirely, not only man's body from his soul, but to separate man from God.

That the spirit and the body should separate . . . is only tolerated for the sake of a reunion, through the grander union of the *Theanthropos* [God-Man] with man.

It is a solemn thing to face death – nothing but a sight of death will meet death.

If . . . there be no escape from sin, there is no escape from death.

On Carlyle's hero-worship: Hero-worship! Ah well, he and I have to meet a strange hero yet – *thanatos* (death) – the greatest that I know of, next to him who overcame him.

Its Origin

What is it that makes death and judgment so terrible? It is sin.

It is not . . . the debt of nature; it is the appointment of God (*Heb.* 9:27).

Of Believers

When godly men are taken away, Christ's prayer is fulfilled, 'that they be with me where I am, that they may behold my glory'.

'They that sleep in Jesus' – beautiful words! beautiful company! From this word of her Lord the church has borrowed her beautiful epithet 'cemetery' [sleeping place].

Jesus died – believers sleep.

I would be glad to go if the Lord would give me Simeon's dismissal: Christ in my arms.

We die not to death; we die to the Lord, to whom we live.

The King of glory has conquered the king of terrors.

We are not death's . . . but we were death's.

On the death of a believer: Yesterday, with me – today, with the Lord! How near heaven seems to be brought!

Comfort from Christ's death: He was in Paradise God and man; he was in the grave God and man.

Regarding the death of his infant daughter: A beautiful female child entered the world with a sigh, breathed (and scarcely breathed) once or twice the atmosphere of this sinful, polluted world, and hastened to appear before God, who keepeth covenant for ever.

Exhortations

Let us contemplate that death in view of the life that is beyond death.

Is death becoming more pleasant? Are you getting any nearer the mind of being willing to depart and to be with Christ?

DESPONDENCY

There is in the farther course of some Christians, that which is the counterpart of the Slough of Despond at the commencement of it. There were cartloads of gospel encouragements cast into the Slough of Despond, and yet it was the Slough of Despond still; and so into this there are carted distinctions and marks of saving grace, yet it remains the counterpart of the Slough of Despond still. There is no dealing with such persons; for if you give them signs of grace, they will ask for signs of the signs.

DEVILS OR DEMONS

I believe there may be more devils than men. They are legion and go in companies.

I think each temptation that assaults a man may be from a separate devil.

No single heart-secret is known to any single devil.

The devil-worship of the East is not worship but fear.

The devils will not be condemned for rejecting the Saviour – just for breach of law.

DEVOTION TO GOD

What's devotion? Is it the seeking to gather in and to gain and to get? It's the going out, the desire to give, whilst the sinner's consciousness that he hath nothing worthy only humbles him, makes it appear an infinite favour if God will take him.

Dr Duncan's advice to William C. Burns on his departure for China: Take you care of his cause, and he will take care of your interests; look after his glory, and he will look after your comfort.

DOCTRINE

Doctrine is just the mind of God as seen in the facts.

Doctrines must rest either on the express affirmations of texts, or be an induction from the comparison of several texts, or an 'analogy of faith' founded on the main scope and bearing of Holy Scripture taken as a whole.

The gospel doctrine is a historic doctrine. It rests on a historic basis. Have your minds resting on a historic basis on the Old Testament predictions and the New Testament fulfilments.

All Christian doctrine is in its tendency of a practical nature.

Must be Sound

Man requires food, the newborn child requires milk, but then neither . . . will nourish them while taken along with poison.

Terrifying Doctrines

In preaching these doctrines never go beyond what can be proved by the express words of the Bible.

Doctrinal Error and Heresy

As the heresies exist, doctrinal teaching is a necessity.

No error is trifling, for every error displaces some truth.

The errors of godly men are the most dangerous.

All error is not heresy.

All errors are abused truths.

Pelagianism, or self-conversion: This heresy, like most others, may be traced back to the first heresy – the heresy of the heart.

DOUBTS AND DOUBTING

There is no doubting in faith; there may be much doubting in the believer.

In him who desires union to the Lord first above all things, doubt of forgiveness is agonizing to himself and dishonouring to Christ.

To one who doubted the genuineness of her faith: Ask yourself (i) How should I feel if the gospel were not true? (ii) What would I take to give up Christ?

I have much sympathy with doubts which arise from a high estimate of Christian character.

There are, it is to be feared, those who by a latent Popery, 'the pride which apes humility', make their doubts a part, and no small part, of their religion.

Spoken to a fellow elder: Many people are anxious to get rid of their doubts; but that old woman that keeps your house, it would be great matter if you could get a doubt dinted [that is, knocked] into her!

Dr Duncan's Own Doubting

Well, if I were sure of heaven, there is nothing I would like better than to depart and be with Christ.

I have not come to the conviction that he will not save me; I believe that he is able, and I have not concluded that he is unwilling.

I can get no deliverance except by acquiescing in the justice of God in my reprobation.

I am naturally of a sceptical turn of mind, and since I have been delivered from doubt about God and the great truths of redemption, my scepticism has taken the form of doubt about my own salvation.

There is a fighting within me between faith and unbelief. I find that I cannot do now without assurance, but I am very unwilling to count myself a believer. I cannot lay hold of the promises. I was trying to read the newspaper, but I loathed everything except thoughts of God and Christ.

My fearfulness is not all from the law, it is from the gospel. The gospel, and that just when I could seek to embrace it, detects sin, detects unbelief, detects the carnal mind – that I am not willing to be saved in God's way.

Alas, I feel that I am not able for continuous study. If I were applying for licence I would not be passed; if I were applying to be made a B.A. I would not be passed; I could not stand an examination in the Grammar School, in Geography and Mathematics . . . I hope in the Lord that that be not fulfilled of me: 'The candle of the wicked shall be put out.'

I am sure that Jesus is the Christ, but I am not sure that I am a Christian.

I have never had any doubts about the truths of Christianity, about the sufficiency of Christ's atonement: my doubts have been about my interest in him, whether I were truly united to him.

To a friend who tried to comfort him with the promise 'When thou passest through the waters', etc.: What makes you so confident about me? You cannot search the heart like God – is my Christianity so very apparent?

DUTY

The creature's first duty is to be what God made him. His next duty is to do what God ordains.

First of all, it is our duty not to have any sin.

ELECTION

To leave out election [from preaching] is to leave out the key-stone of the arch.

The whole spring of salvation is in God's election; but this stream of salvation flows out before us in a free gospel; and we are to drink at the water, not at the fountain-head, but as it flows by us, yet acknowledging the fountain from which it flows.

2 Peter 1:10: It is only through the calling that the election is made sure. The election, as regards God's part, is at the foundation of the calling: the calling, as regards man's knowledge, is at the foundation of the election.

The Lord has not revealed the names of the elect saved, but he has revealed the name of the elect Saviour.

Evidence of Election

Now where we find sanctification of the Spirit, and obedience, and sprinkling of the blood of Jesus Christ, we need question election no more.

THE ENGLISH LANGUAGE

The English is really a most noble language, capable of expressing almost anything, if men only knew its capabilities and the secret of its strength and beauty.

ENVY AND VAUNTING

Envy is an unhappy feeling with regard to the good of our neighbour, a desire that he should be stripped of it and we put in possession of it, and, if that do not take place, then a grudge.

Vaunting has reference to the good which I have got, and my neighbour has not. The envy looks at what he has got, and the vaunting looks at what I have got, and he has not.

EVANGELICALISM

When I was an atheist, I used to feel that if the Evangelic system were only true it was worth a man's believing; but even if the Moderate[1] system were true, it was not worth believing.

EVANGELISM

God has made us evangelists to the world.

You have got the sinner's gospel, and if you have it, it is to give to sinners.

Men evangelized cannot go to hell but over the bowels of God's mercies.

EXPERIENCE

Not even experience is always a successful teacher; some are such fools that they will not learn even in that school.

FAITH

Faith is at once receptive and operative . . . Faith is purely receptive. Yet not only does it produce our good works, it is an operative principle, and there is a labouring in it.

[1]The Moderate party in the Church of Scotland combined a sympathy for liberal scholarship, a distrust of Puritan piety and an aversion to the Calvinism of the Westminster Confession.

The faith of adherence may not be a very strong thing; it is not assurance, but it is a very tenacious thing; it cleaves to the Lord against solicitations alluring it away, and against discouragements from the Lord himself.

Faith, trust for salvation, is worship – there cannot be higher worship than the surrender of one's whole nature, body and soul, the understanding and conscience and will, to another.

Whatever God can do, that, in the name of Christ, may I ask him to do, and depend that he will do.

Its Objects

Divine faith hath reference to all manifestations God makes, and therefore it includes natural as well as revealed religion.

Faith takes all the words of God.

We are called to exercise faith, but we are not called to look in on faith as a condition; we are called to exercise faith in looking out on the unmixed promise of God, which yet can be received only by believers.

It is on report that faith goes.

Christ in Scripture: Ah! What an object this is for faith to gaze on – his glory as exhibited in Scripture testimony!

Our faith and hope are in Christ Jesus . . . because he is God . . . But . . . our faith does not terminate on him, but goes on through him to God the Father.

Faith has been well defined [by Andrew Gray] as a continual travelling between our own emptiness and Christ's fulness.

Faith receives Christ as a whole Christ, not for justification merely, but for salvation, which includes it.

However weak explicitly in some relations, in its implicit act it receives (1) His Person as God-man and Saviour of sinners; (2) His function of Mediator; and (3) His offices of Prophet, Priest and King.

Faith receives Christ lovingly; faith, not love; yet not without love, but lovingly.

Faith receives a beloved Christ.

Faith is an imperfect medium of communion with Christ. It is a true medium . . . yet it is an imperfect medium.

However different the life of sight in the glorified is from the life of faith in the justified, their principle is the same – beholding the glory of Christ.

Living by Faith

We must live the life of faith now – faith wide as the Word of God, and narrow as the Word of God.

God has a right to a full, an undoubting, unhesitating faith.

Believers live not on the first act of their faith, but on the continual act of their faith; because it is not faith they live on, but Christ.

In the life of faith, it is conjugal faith and love and obedience toward Christ, and filial faith and love and obedience toward God.

We can no more live by yesterday's faith than we can see by yesterday's light, or have our life supported by yesterday's food.

There is no right practice unless it is founded on faith.

In the life of faith, distinguish between taking faith and giving faith . . . Let Christ have the greater blessedness of giving.

Faith and Reason

I think faith has the start of reason from the first . . . though it is a power, it is a barren power, which can produce nothing till revelation descends to meet it.

When you come down with the lamp of faith into the sphere of reason, you perceive some truths that you saw not before.

It's a poor faith that cannot stand against many unsolved difficulties.

Its Place in the Order of Salvation

Faith precedes justification, but regeneration . . . precedes faith.

Its Imperfection

I believe there may be God-made faith and man-made faith in the same soul.

Faith's view of Christ is transforming, is glorifying. But it is not so transforming, not so glorifying, as the vision of immediate presence.

Faith at its brightest is dim compared with sight.

There may be some true faith incrusted with a vast deal of presumption.

Faith and Repentance

Faith and repentance are inseparable twins. Woe unto the faith which kills repentance! Woe unto that repentance which kills faith!

It is only through divine teaching that anyone, child or grown-up man, can apprehend what it is to believe and to repent. With that teaching the youngest child can understand as well as the philosopher.

Faith and Unbelief

Whenever faith sees a thing in God's hand, then faith says, 'I have it'; but when unbelief sees it, it says, 'Ah, then I need never expect it!'

The Misuse of Faith

Some men's Trinity consists of the Father, and the Son, and Faith.

False Faith

There may be a certain buoyancy and happiness which is

a delusion. It is my desire to nip in the bud that flimsy hope which now so commonly passes for faith.

Reminders, Warnings and Encouragements

He who produces faith, tries it.

Was faith crucified for you; or were ye baptized in the name of faith?

We may hang a dead work on a dead faith.

Don't make faith a cloak for sin.

Faith, both in the true and the false, seems rapidly giving way.

Ah! in the darkest night of this world there are no stars; but in the darkest night in the soul there is ever the light of the things unseen and eternal.

If ye cannot behold him distinctly as the Object of faith, behold Jesus as the Author of faith.

FAMILY WORSHIP

I insist very strongly on Christian teaching in the household, and on the necessity of stated family worship.

We are Romish if we substitute the church service for the altar at home.

I would insist on family worship being at once established. Willingness to begin it, and to prefer it to excited meetings, is a good criterion.

FASTING

Fasting is a duty, an extraordinary one.

FEAR

'The fear of the Lord' (*Psa.* 128:1) – there is an aspect common to all religion, and therefore to all dispensations.

Fear [is] the summary of Old Testament religion. Faith is more characteristic of the New Testament, but fear is not excluded now.

Beware of base timidity.

FEELINGS

Some feelings are too big for words.

Shallow feeling generally expresses itself in pompous language; that which is deeper in the plainest and simplest words; but that which is deepest can find no language to express it.

FLATTERY

Oh, beware of flatterers; beware of the flatteries of Christians.

FREE WILL

It is foolish to dismiss the question of free will as an insoluble problem of metaphysics. Let no man despise a metaphysical problem.

The will is a metaphysical question . . . though it is also a practical question, vitally practical.

The liberty which is the ground of accountability is more than freedom from restraint . . . It is less than the liberty of independency and . . . indifference.

I disown the liberty of independence. I disown the liberty of indifference . . . I disown the freedom from co-action without the will (external bondage), and freedom from co-action within the will (internal bondage).

Independency [of will] is just Epicureanism.

Men talk much of their own free-will and independence. Men scoff at spiritual influence, but every man is under it.

To become truly free, we need to be emancipated from . . . lawlessness, which is slavery.

In a certain sense, I am a tremendous free-willer. My predestination is all free will!

FRIENDSHIP

He whom we admit into our friendship, we admit into the formation of our character.

GENIUS

Genius lies very much in that region where the profound is simple and the simple is profound.

Carey was sneeringly called 'The Sanctified Cobbler'. But God has plenty of talent down in the understrata of society which he can bring up if he please.

GLORY

God is a glorious God – Christ is a glorious Christ – the salvation which is in Christ Jesus with eternal glory is a very glorious object.

There are things unseen and eternal, and there are men and women looking at them, who under the light of them, brighter than ten thousand stars, are marching on through afflictions, trials and temptations, unto them. There is a land of holiness, of peace, of joy, of love. There, the Holy Ghost filling every soul born of him and nourished of him, the spirit born of the Spirit basks eternally in the contemplation of the divine glory and excellence and love.

GOD

His Existence

I first saw clearly the existence of God in walking along the bridge in Aberdeen; it was a great discovery to me; I stopped and stood in an ecstasy of joy at seeing the existence of God. I stood and thanked God for his existence.

When I was convinced that there was a God, I danced on the Brig o' Dee with delight.

There is a God, there is a God; Jehovah he is the God, Jehovah he is the God.

Ah! What is God? That is a solemn question – and none of us can attempt such an answer as will exhaust the thing and satisfy.

As for a logical proof of the divine existence, I am convinced that when the faith is more than parrotism and traditionalism, the Spirit of God has had more to do with it than some orthodox divines are willing to admit.

The belief in God presses multifariously upon man . . . It is not here or there; it is everywhere.

His Nature

God is life, and God is light, and God is love.

God is a lovely Being.

Man is like unto God, made in his image, but God is also infinitely unlike man.

His Name

If God were nameless, he could not be loved.

His Glory

What is glory? It is the harmony of the divine perfections of Jehovah.

Make him glorious we cannot; but think how glorious he is, and tell how glorious he is . . . we may.

Not only is God glorious, but all glory belongs to him.

The only way not to glory before him is to glory in him.

Triune

The Trinity is my highest *theologoumenon*. I reach it and find in it the supreme harmony of revealed things. But it is equally irrational and irreverent to speculate on the nexus between the Persons. This is not revealed, and I think is not revealable.

No good thought originates with us, but from the blessed Trinity in us.

The Father is a name of endearment, but this Father is very venerable.

I do not believe in any direct vision of the Father in the future, except as through the Son, and with the Son.

His Attributes Made Known

There would certainly have been no display of some of the divine attributes had sin not been. They would have been conserved for ever in the depths of the adorable Godhead.

What infinite condescension that he should say, 'There are my excellencies, O my creature – sinful, redeemed, bought and called – there are my excellencies for thee to contemplate, for thee to adore . . . for thee to trust in, for thee to love, for thee to imitate.'

The divine perfections do not necessitate any act, but they qualify and condition every divine act.

Shorter Sayings

His Blessedness

The blessed Jehovah was blessed in himself before his creatures were in existence.

His Infinity

There would come a time in eternity when we would be tired of the enjoyment of God, if there was not an infinity in him.

There can be no ladder to the infinite.

Eternal and Unchangeable

God . . . cannot die.

We can be only in the present, but not in the present without a past, nor in the present without a future. We need a present stretching from an eternal past and to an eternal future. In Jehovah alone is such a past, present and future found (*Psa.* 90:1–2).

We cannot tell what all things are, and what things may be, but we know what he is . . . unchangeably good, wise, holy, gracious, just – and that suffices.

Though our lives be to us uncertain, nothing is uncertain to God.

Change what may, he is unchangeable.

The causing of a change does not imply a change in the Causer of it.

Omnipresent

The eternal Jehovah is not only near thee, with thee – he is *in* thee! in thee in all his almightiness!

We live within God's omnipresence.

Omniscient

'He looketh upon men' . . . his unceasing, judicial omniscience.

Many words are spoken, and God, as omniscient, hears them all.

Everything that is done is photographed . . . The great Photographer records our acts, and preserves the record.

Holy

Holiness . . . is an essential attribute of God, whereby his blessed nature is infinitely contrary to all moral evil, and infinitely resplendent in all moral good.

The holiness that is in God . . . infinite, spotless, moral excellence and beauty.

A holy God must have holy people.

O my holy One, thou art of purer eyes than to behold iniquity! Is Jupiter like that? Is Brahma like that? Oh, the vanities of the heathen!

Jehovah is contradistinguished from all false gods by his being holy.

God is a holy God, and so his place is a holy place: his temple is a holy temple, his people are holy people, his land is a holy land, and his service a holy service.

A holy God and an unholy people cannot consort. He can have no pleasure in them, nor they any pleasure in him.

Just

It is a righteous thing in God to mark iniquity. It is against him . . . the holiness of his nature . . . the rectitude of his will . . . the equity of his law . . . the whole principle of his moral government.

Would it be an unjust thing if God were to damn you?

In his acts of judgment, in his acts as judge, God deals with every man according to his character.

If penal suffering have any existence, it has its origin in vindictive justice.

Punitive justice, or the infliction of misery on the creature due to his sin, is ascribed to God in the Holy Scriptures. It must be ascribed to him, else other principles must be adopted to account for misery – namely, the ascription of malevolence to God.

May God . . . keep us both from contempt of his justice and despair of his mercy.

God is to be viewed by us – faith views him – as he reveals himself in all that strict justice, and in all that tenderness and amplitude of forgiveness.

Good

How good God is! he bids everybody love me! 'Thou shalt love thy neighbour as thyself.'

God [is] liberal, yet economical of his gifts.

When shall we learn that God is a bountiful Giver?

God is very good to you, so good that he wishes everyone to love you.

A prayer regarding God's goodness: O Lord Jehovah, do me all the good thou canst; whatever blessings thou canst bestow, empty thy goodness on me, on mine, on thy church, on the world.

Merciful

There could not be the exercise of mercy till there was misery; but God was always a merciful God.

We owe God a debt of praise even for those mercies which we have squandered.

Mercy . . . it flows to misery . . . but it flows at mercy's free will. 'I will have mercy on whom I will have mercy.' It is not by the attraction of the misery, but by the free-will motion of mercy toward misery.

Mercy has an open door.

Mercy will pardon and bless – and truth will proclaim and insure (*Psa.* 85:10).

After sharp rebukes in truth and faithfulness, it is sweet to hear again the voice – not the words only – the voice of infinitely condescending mercy, grace and love.

Chesed, rendered 'mercy' (*Psa.* 130:7), is the peculiar affection which Jehovah bears to Israel as related to him.

Mercy must ever be sovereign.

The man who would rest content with God's mercy at some future time is the man who is content to rest without it.

God's mercy, grace, compassion . . . are infinite, un-bounded – an infinite ocean.

It is not enough for the sinner that God is a merciful God; he must have a merciful purpose.

Gracious

Grace is not founded on the atonement; the atonement is founded on grace. The atonement is God's device through which his grace, self-moving, can flow forth, reigning through righteousness unto eternal life by Jesus Christ our Lord. The atonement did not make God propitious, merciful, longsuffering, but God's great love said, 'I am ready to forgive, if I can do it justly', and his infinite wisdom finding that he could do it justly this way, he resolved on the sacrifice, on this way to it. 'Herein is love, not that we loved God, but that he loved us' – the gift of his Son is the fruit of the love – 'and sent his Son to be the propitiation for our sins'.

Grace is necessary, and it is sovereign.

The position of believers, as children, is not founded on obedience, but grace.

God is gracious to the need; he will not be . . . indulgent to the sloth.

The righteousness through which grace reigns, grace provides.

Loving

Jehovah's love is wondrous because it is to those who did not love.

Till we . . . have been enabled to reach to the knowledge of this love, we have . . . no idea of what love is.

Undoubtedly the divine love does and cannot but embrace all God's sentient creatures, as such. I doubt not that God has a Creator's heart to fallen spirits.

The Creator's heart is infinitely more loving than all the sum of love that has ever been in the heart of creatures towards creatures.

Jealous

A jealous God is at least not a God careless about us. He sets store by our love. When we squander our love upon vanities, he is jealous.

Isaiah 42:13: Jealousy makes heroic war.

Faithful

He has not forsaken the earth, though the earth has forsaken him.

Men forget God their Maker; God forgets not men.

Truthful

Let us see to it that every declaration of the Lord Jehovah be as firmly believed by us as it is truthfully spoken by him.

Sovereign

Beyond astronomers' conceptions as well as calculations . . . remains the throne of the eternal God.

The throne of the eternal God still stands.

It becomes not us to seek to dictate to infinite goodness, acting sovereignly in infinite wisdom. He may do what he will with his own.

We must be alone with God in order to learn that he is God.

Omnipotent

In his divine omnipotence [God] is invested with a natural dominion over all possibles.

God's *energeia* is not galvanism; it is a vitalising act.

I've sometimes thought that God's greatest power is best seen in the most silent awakenings of the spirit of man.

His Thoughts

Psalm 44:11; 92:5; 139:17; Isaiah 55:8; Jeremiah 29:11: I feel that in those great and good thoughts of God, from which I would fain draw mine, there is all life and wealth.

God has reason, but he does not reason.

His Perfection

He is more perfect than we can conceive.

The moral perfection of God . . . is indestructible.

It is . . . fundamental in theology that creation was for the manifestation of the divine perfection.

His Majesty

Oh, what mercy in that frown, however awful and terrible, by which the Lord vindicates his majesty, holiness, justice; filling the soul with approving dread, and laying it low at his feet. And then when he is heard saying, 'This is my beloved Son, hear ye him', and when our eye meets the Father's eye fixed on his Son, oh, how the divine majesty, holiness and justice become the full brightness of Jehovah the Father's smile; and it reaches us both by reflection and direct transmission.

His Incomprehensibility

There is a mystery about the doctrine of God which we would need ourselves to be God to know, and the light of glory will not dissipate that mystery.

The things of God are too big for me.

His Will

It is a solemn thing that we and all creatures are at the disposal of pure will; but it is not merely free will; it is the free will of the holy Lord Jehovah, and therein it is distinguished from the abstractness and apparent arbitrariness of mere will.

It is a holy will that rules the universe – a will in which lovingkindness is locked up, to be in due time displayed.

He does not, cannot, will, but according to his own faithful promise and loving heart.

Knowing God

Our knowledge of the infinite Object may not be adequate, yet true and sufficient.

God must be anthropomorphic . . . in his communications. He tells us that he is infinitely unlike us; but when he is to speak to man, he must do so anthropomorphically.

Our knowledge of God is apprehensive, never comprehensive; but it is real and presentative, not ideal and representative.

All light is from the Father of lights.

One who may be afraid to call God his Father may betray it [that is, his sonship] by running to God, when the strait comes, to do for him a Father's part. The spirit of the relation flows from the fact of the relation.

To know that Jehovah is God is to know his character and perfections as revealed in his Word and his corresponding works.

The hope in men of renewed rectitude, tranquillity and joy when they have been lost, is just . . . the knowledge that Jehovah is God.

A test of our knowledge: Only that which comes from God will lead to God.

I do think (would that I were sure) that the thought of being without God in the world is abhorrent to my heart.

Loving God

I would be bound to love God for what he is in himself, even while his very nature was inflicting punishment on myself.

Men cannot love a God that is misunderstood.

Obligation to this duty is not founded upon grace. Inclination to discharge this duty does come of grace, but obligation to discharge it does not come of grace, but of eternal and immutable law, as founded on the eternal loveliness of God.

Not to love God! That is the crime of crimes and shame of shames.

Who can tell the hatefulness of not loving God?

Oh! I can't endure to hate God any longer.

I pray the Lord my God to circumcise my heart to love the Lord my God, to love him for his own essential, revealed excellencies, with devoted love; that the Beloved (O my soul, O Spirit of the Lord, is he or is he not my Beloved?) may be mine, and I his, and I his, and I his.

Enjoying God

Shorter Catechism, Answer 1: I pass over the first part mainly with an intellectual approbation of its moral rectitude as a requirement, 'Man's chief end is to glorify God'; while every fibre of my soul winds itself round the latter part, 'to enjoy him for ever', with unutterable, sickening, fainting desire.

What a God! What a God have I! What a source of blessedness!

God's being a God to anyone implies his doing all that a God can do.

The heart which faints with the very longing is strengthened for the enjoyment.

. . . to hold the great God in the little heart of man!

God and his People

Between God and his people there is a special relation. He is their God and they are his people. He is their chosen God and they are his chosen people. And the question only is, 'With whom did this mutual choice begin? With him or with them?' Ah, their choice is just their approach. 'Blessed is the man whom thou choosest, and causest to approach unto thee' (*Psa.* 65:4).

A Solemn Question

What evil has God done you? . . . What good has the devil done you?

GODLINESS

Oh, there is no sweetness in any life like a godly life – a life of spiritual joys – of joyous, solemn faith in the Son of God.

I believe there would be much more of that honeymoon in Christians if they maintained a close walk with God.

The deepest life of godliness may co-exist with muddled doctrine. But this is no argument in favour of obscurity.

GOODNESS

The homage which the bad give to the principle of goodness is . . . seen in this, that bad men almost always wish their children to be good.

'Scarcely for a righteous man will one die: yet peradventure for a good man some would even dare to die' (*Rom.* 5:7). It is a saying of one of the Rabbins, 'He who says, Mine is mine and thine is thine, is a righteous man; he who says, Mine is mine and thine is mine, is a wicked man; but he who says, Thine is thine and mine is thine, is a good man.'

God we maintain to be the Author of good, of all good, and of good only.

GOOD WORKS

Christ does not ask, 'What think ye more than others?', but, 'What do ye more than others?'

GOSPEL

The gospel contains the doctrine of salvation and the sinner's warrant to believe.

What is the gospel? It is the declaration of God's wondrous love.

The gospel is a prepared feast for unprepared guests.

The gospel is not a mere remedial system. Christ came into the world that we might have life, and that we might have it more abundantly.

The gospel is all Christology together.

I have never heard the gospel better stated than it was put by a poor negress: 'Me die, or he die: he die, me no die.'

That everlasting gospel brings before you an everlasting Saviour, one who is 'able to save them to perpetuity that come unto God by him'.

The gospel is enlightening and enriching.

The rest which Jesus gives to the weary and heavy laden, as soon as they come to him, taking their heavy yoke and burden *off*, is found by them when they take his light yoke and burden *on*.

Oh, what a light does the gospel shed!

To be Preached

The gospel is needed equally by every man; it is adapted to every man; by God's appointment it is to be preached to every man under heaven.

Mind you have got the sinner's gospel . . . faith rests on the sinner's gospel. There you begin; there you must end. If you had only a saint's gospel, what would that do for sinners?

You can tell sinners that you are not more welcome to Christ than they are, that you have no better gospel than they have got.

In Relation to the Law

The sum of God's law is, 'Thou shalt love'; the sum of God's gospel is, 'God so loved'. Wherefore, let the law of love be in your heart and your life.

The gospel . . . interferes not with, nor sets aside, any claim of God's holy and righteous law.

The gospel brings us back to the law.

The gospel is that he will multiply to pardon, but will not take down his demands.

False Gospel Identifiable

It is easy to invite rebels to return to God, if there be a keeping out of view of the cause of the quarrel between the rebels and God.

It needs no regeneration to believe it, but it needs regenerating grace to make a man unable to believe it.

Easy Believism

I think that gospel encouragements are too hurriedly and lightly snatched at. They are designed to meet certain weighty considerations, and if such are absent, the encouragement is not truly received at all.

Its Warrant

Not in anything in ourselves naturally, or wrought in us by the power of the Holy Ghost, is found the ground, the warrant to receive Jesus Christ – but in the free offer of the gospel.

In believing on Christ, we do it not on the ground of any speciality, but on the ground of that which is common to us with mankind.

It is in the gospel that Christ is offered, and that is the warrant of our faith.

We must beware of substituting any other warrant for trusting in Christ than the gospel.

The work of the Spirit – in convincing, enlightening, enabling to believe in Christ – must never be put as our warrant to believe on Christ.

Christ is the object of saving faith, and God in him. The Spirit is the efficient cause, the word of the truth of the gospel is the warrant.

The gospel does not address convinced sinners as such with offers of reconciliation, but fallen sinners.

A sinner convinced is no more entitled to believe by his being convinced than an unconvinced sinner.

If only convinced sinners are warranted to embrace Christ, then I must, ere I can be warranted to embrace him, be convinced that I am a convinced sinner. But the Holy Spirit is the only source of infallible conviction, and the Holy Spirit is nowhere promised to convict of conviction; he is only promised to convince of sin.

Wherever the gospel is preached, all may, in point of warrant, 'behold the Lamb of God'. But few do. And the aggravation of the majority's ruin is that all may.

The Free Offer

What is offered is not a doctrine but a Person.

It is Christ that is offered. He is freely offered. It is in the gospel that he is freely offered.

The offer of Christ more than makes up for the Fall.

In the everlasting gospel the invitation is addressed to all.

Calvinism is not inconsistent with a free gospel.

The gospel is not a mere offer, it is an imperative offer. The surgeon of a regiment does not merely offer his help to the wounded soldier; the man has no right to remain sick, or to refuse to receive the doctor. The fellow must get his knee cured, that he may not have to be discharged, but get well and serve his Queen. So, the gospel does not say, 'There is a Saviour, if you wish to be saved'; but, 'Sir, you have no right to go to hell – you can't go there without trampling on the Son of God.'

Everyone here is welcome to enter into the favour of God.

All are invited, all are commanded.

Oh, how self-condemned must the man be who says that the gospel is true, and the gospel is free, and saying that, stays away from God!

Whether you can reconcile the free invitations of the gospel with God's absolute decrees or not, nothing is more plain than that these invitations are most free.

'Him that cometh unto me I will in no wise cast out.' Who can count the numbers who have trusted upon that word, and none of them has been disappointed?

Christ is 'freely offered to us in the gospel' (Shorter Catechism, Answer to Question 31) . . . Have you the pledge of the Offerer in that or not? . . . No, the Offerer is not pledged by the offer, but he is pledged when the offer is accepted.

Christ is offered in the gospel, presented to you for your present acceptance; therefore you have all in free offer – Christ and all his benefits for present and immediate acceptance.

Such as we are, Christ tells us that he is willing to have us; he will take us as we are. But we are ever trying to come as we are not . . . so he shows us what we are.

Sinner, take Christ, you will get everything.

Reception of Christ is reception by faith, which works by love.

He is . . . your own in the free offer of God.

After hearing a sermon on Isaiah 55:1: When I heard all the good things that were offered in this market, I said to myself, 'I will marry the merchant and they will all be mine.'

Exhortations, Warnings and Encouragements

Listen to his own invitation. Oh, cherish his own invitation.

Look. You say you cannot, but 'Look, ye blind' – he bids you.

Now, how long, oh, how long, shall the meat which is set before you on the gospel table . . . be left untasted by you?

If we perish under the gospel, it is that we preferred sin to salvation by Christ.

Oh, you have nothing that you have half such a right to lay hold of as Christ.

GRACE

The transition from grace to glory is not greater than is the transition from nature to grace.

Why do we coop up divine grace within narrow man-made channels, and say, This is the way God has worked and will work?

All grace keeps man dependent upon God.

Let no man take for granted that he has grace irrespective of the exercise of gracious affections.

If . . . you have tasted that the Lord is gracious, have tasted the grace by personal experience, by the reception of it on testimony, it is sweet to you (*1 Pet.* 2:3).

I cannot give a better mark by which to examine ourselves than one which I have found in Halyburton's memoir, a book which I would recommend to your serious study. After examining himself with regard to the law, taking – as it were wise in us to do – himself at his worst time. Well, he found at his worst time, and with regard to the law at his worst time, 'I never wish the law to be changed to meet my heart; but that my heart may be changed to meet God's law'. Can we at our worst time say so? If so, to us bondage has become a law of liberty.

Humbling in its Effect

There is nothing so humbling as grace. A load of sin weighs down the soul crushingly: a load of benefits makes it stoop gratefully.

Imparted to Form Gracious Character

When grace imparted symmetrically pervades the whole character, there is not only life but beauty.

The strength of any principle is to be estimated not merely by the other effects that it produces, but also by the resistance it has to overcome [quoting Riccaltoun of Hobkirk with approval].

In some persons grace manifests itself towards God in the closet, and towards man in great conscientiousness.

If he is willing to receive great service, he is willing to give great grace.

It is only by daily communications out of the fulness of Christ Jesus that we are able to meet any danger or to get through any work in such a manner as to glorify God and to be profitable to our own souls and the souls of others.

Its Reward

If you have given aught to him [that is, Christ], he will not only thank but reward you with the reward – Oh, mark and mind this! – not of merit but of grace.

From Grace to Glory

There is what Toplady calls 'The Euthanasia' – the happy death of faith and hope. Faith, when perfected, expires; sight takes place. And hope, when perfected, expires; fruition takes place. But love perfected continues.

We should be thankful for God's gracious bestowments, but he docs not require us to be satisfied till in the morning we be satisfied with his likeness.

HATRED

A life of hatred is a life of sin.

Hatred is death.

Hateful haters! A world of hateful haters!

We were not lovers, because we were haters. But love could overcome that.

HEART

It is so wide a thing that God alone in all his fulness can fill a human heart.

Oh, the human heart . . . is a wide thing; it can hold much; it can hold apparent contrarieties. It can hold great joy along with heaviness, provided they flow from different sources.

Many men's hearts are better than their heads, and many men add their own inferences to the teaching of the Spirit of God when but a very little part of them may be his teaching.

The loving heart gives keenness to the eyes.

I delight in the law of God after the inner man; but some men have no inner man.

Warnings

Beware of resting short of giving the whole heart unto God . . . We must give God the wicked heart.

Oh, beware of judicial blindness and hardness of heart!

HEAVEN

Heaven is a glorious place, and there are glorious beings in it.

Heaven is a place of perfected love.

The believer has his eye on a heaven of rest; it is a heaven of love.

There is a land of holiness, of peace, of joy, of love. There . . . the spirit born of the Spirit basks eternally in the contemplation of the divine glory and excellence of love.

I am quite persuaded that the occupations of time will have an influence on the occupations of eternity, that they will be in the same train.

The inheritance is not of our procuring nor of our keeping; he who procured it for us keeps it for us.

1 Peter 1:5: It is kept for you, and you for it . . . You are in an enemy's country yet . . . but you are garrisoned.

Friends, God hath provided an eternal heaven for us in his own Lamb. He is Heaven's heaven.

Christ the centre of heaven: The eyes of the glorified shall through eternity rest on this Object [that is, the Lamb].

Only for the holy: A holy God and an unholy sinner, an angry God and a guilty sinner, would not make a happy heaven together.

How believers enter heaven: We shall enter as conscious sinners, but with consciences at peace with God through Christ.

I have all my life been hanging about the doors, but I have not yet gone in. I think we may be content to remain still at the door a little longer; a little longer, till we're done with the darkness.

HELL

It is a terrible thought that a man might be left to the agony of his own reminiscence for ever.

Hell is no blot in God's universe.

A prayer: If thou shouldst now cast me into hell, all holy beings would say, 'Righteous art thou, O Lord, when thou judgest.'

HISTORY

History is the unfolding of the mystery of God.

HOLINESS

Holiness and happiness can be found only in God.

The pursuit of holiness as so much personal adornment is a very subtle snare.

THE HOLY SPIRIT

We cannot rightly think that the influences of the Spirit were purchased by Christ . . . [They are] the unpurchasable blessings of grace.

We live under the Pentecostal economy of the Holy Ghost; what was done that day was but the opening scene.

The Holy Ghost hath not left his omnipotence behind. He is not omnipotent in heaven and impotent in you.

I believe there is such a thing as the local presence of the Spirit.

The Spirit of Christ

The Holy Ghost in this Pentecostal dispensation is what he could not be before: the Spirit of a glorified Saviour.

In Relation to the Word

The Word is nothing without the Spirit.

HOPE

Spiritual hope is a grace; and where you will find a 'perhaps' you will find that.

The foundation of our hope is without us – the lively hope produced by God is within.

There is hope of a man as long as he is out of hell . . . and fear of a man as long as he is out of heaven.

HUMILITY

A lowly place befits one so degraded.

On Romans 12:3: But God does not require of us a false humility. We are not to think less highly of ourselves than we ought to think. We are to think soberly. We are to find out the truth about ourselves, and think that, and then there will be no danger of our thinking too highly.

He [that is, Christ] brings us down . . . to the deeper humility of not refusing the offer because of unmeetness – the deepest humility I know of.

Dr Duncan's Humility

I am not well acquainted with the history of Jesus Christ.

I know about Christ second-hand from Paul.

I have been taken up with systems, and do not know the letter of Scripture.

Wednesday 9 February 1870 (two weeks before his death): Oh, how darkly I see through a glass! And how I have neglected the great salvation! I thank the Lord for a hope of his salvation; but I see that if I had lived more closely with him, it had been better now. Salvation is entirely of grace; yet God makes, as it were, gracious compensation to those who seek him, and most to those who seek him most. I do not say that I do not know him and his great salvation – no; but, Oh, John Duncan! you might have been a better man at the end of this life than you are, though it is as a sinner deserving to perish you must lie down and die, were you the very best.

HYPER-CALVINISTS

John Gill is the greatest of them; he best systemised it; and I believe that John Gill loved holiness, just as I believe that John Wesley trusted in grace.

Mere evangelism sets before men an open door, but when you have gone through it you find nothing; there is no house to the door. Ultra-Calvinism is a beautiful palace without a door; the house is perfect, but there is no getting into it.

John Gill I reckon the best, as well as the most learned, of all the Hyper-Calvinists. The rabbinical and the patristic were fairly blended in him. He mistakenly charges us with what he calls 'Duty-Faith', but he was a good and reverent man.

HYPOCRISY AND HYPOCRITES

Seeming without being, acting without being, that is hypocrisy.

It is a sad thing to have the name of anything and not the reality.

Whatever I am, I'm not a hypocrite, and won't be one.

IDOLATRY

If you make an idol of me, there will be no glory to God, you will do yourself no good, and you will do me much harm.

I have been making idols of languages, and God is now saying to me, 'These are thy gods, and as thou hast forsaken me, I will forsake thee.'

I did not duly watch and pray, but yielded to the temptation of my idol linguistics ... And so my heart wickedly was withdrawn from God.

Idolatry is but man's helpless effort to get back to God, in whose image he was made.

INTOLERANCE

The vague, cloudy men are always talking against intolerance. Why, our very calling is to be intolerant; intolerant of proved error and known sin.

JEWS

What was a Jew? An expectant Christian.

The Abrahamic covenant was to them the gospel.

A true Jew was the very opposite of a Pharisee. He was a sinner who knew God.

The 'Israelite indeed' had aweful, reverential impressions of Jehovah's majesty, mysteriousness and holiness.

Oh, that I could get any, any Gentile to know the heart of a Jew!

Abrahamism – the seed of Abraham is the parent-stem of the true faith, and by it of life everlasting for the whole world.

Jehovism – the religion of the Bible as a revelation of God as standing in saving relations to man.

Among my earliest inducements to labour for Israel was my being cheated by a pair of Jews to the tune of £5 . . . people did not know that I allowed myself to be cheated with my eyes open, that I might gain an opportunity of slyly stealing away a prejudice or two, and insinuating a word for him who is the Gentiles' light and Israel's glory.

Jews who have read the New Testament have often said to me, 'It is all very good, but Christians do not believe it themselves – why should Jews?'

Metaphorically, we must all become Jews; that is, we must enter into the Jewish heritage, and reverence the channel in which all our blessings have come down to us.

Jewish Converts in Budapest

They used to read day after day the epistles of Paul as if they had been letters that had come by that morning's post.

Judaism

Judaism was not a missionary but a conservative system, yet there was some provision made for the Gentiles; before the door was wide open it was somewhat ajar.

JOY

Joy that is easily come at – that is not preceded by weeks or months of sadness and sorrow – is of very little worth.

Spiritual joy is a delicate thing; it is easily spoiled; it requires much tenderness.

1 Peter 1:6: The joy . . . is a lasting joy, as lasting as the inheritance.

Unmixed joy, that is not for earth; that hath never been on the earth since Adam fell, unless, perhaps, in the Man of Sorrows, after his resurrection, when the load was off.

Exhortations

If you walk near to God, if you make a good use of your present joy, it may be that you will have less sorrow than many.

Let us seek to abound in . . . reverential fear solemnising all our joy.

Why is it you have not so much joy at seeing the freeness of the gospel, the willingness of Jesus to save you, as you had at first? The gospel is the same; it is as free as ever; therefore the fault must be in yourself. Do not stand still; the door is wide open; you must press in.

JUSTIFICATION
(*see also* SANCTIFICATION)

It is the sentence of God to slay our sins and to save our persons.

A man cannot be justified but as a condemned sinner; and he cannot be justified at the bar of God if he . . . is not also condemned at the bar of conscience.

If God justify the ungodly at all, it is easy to believe that he can justify the most ungodly.

Its Position in Theology

There are fundamentals beneath justification. The Person of Christ is fundamental. Justification, and all else connected with it, is grounded on moral law.

Justification by faith is the meeting-point of many doctrines, a rallying centre of theology; but it is not the foundation doctrine.

Justification and Atonement

In justification God absolves the personally guilty, and in the atonement God inflicts misery on one personally innocent who voluntarily comes in the room of the guilty.

Condemnation of sin to death goes along with the adjudication of persons to life. Christ died for the destruction of sin, but for the salvation of the unjust.

Justification and Sanctification

God in justification imputeth the righteousness of Christ . . . In sanctification his Spirit infuseth holiness . . . In justification sin is pardoned . . . In sanctification it is subdued.

. . . Nor can I ever consider justification and sanctification farther separated than as a legal sentence and the actual execution of it.

That justification precedes sanctification is another of the ultra-isms of modern Protestantism. I cannot receive that doctrine. Faith precedes justification, but regeneration causally precedes faith.

It is the evil extreme of Romanism that it deprives sanctification of its legal grounds; and it is the evil of an ultra-Protestantism that it stops short at the act of justification.

It is a significant fact that the whole Western Church lost the doctrine of justification by faith, from the apostles' days to Luther's by confounding justification with sanctification. Even Augustine, clear and pellucid as he is as to grace, in opposition to Pelagian merit, contemplates grace in us reigning in our sanctification. We learn from this great fact that the deepest life of godliness may co-exist with muddled doctrine. But that is no argument in favour of obscurity.

KINDNESS

We cannot be more philanthropic than the philanthropic Jehovah (*Titus* 3:4).

In affliction, mere natural human kindness is a very valuable communication from the philanthropic God.

KINGS AND PRIESTS

Oh, for more of the kingly life and the priestly life! Oh, for the lowly majesty of the kings, and the consecration of the priests! . . . Oh, for the dignity of the kings and priests, with the lowliness of washed sinners!

KNOWLEDGE

We know only the finite; but in the consciousness of our ability to transcend the finite, we are inspired with a belief in . . . the infinite.

It is something to know that you don't know, still more is it to know what you don't know.

A methodised index to knowledge is a large conception, but no-one can produce it. It is not possible perfectly to classify all that is at this time known.

There is no true knowledge . . . that does not lead to corresponding practice.

LANGUAGE AND LANGUAGES

The more I study language, the more I am convinced of this, that particular shades of thought are wedded to particular words. If you disuse the words, you lose the thought.

I find that my best words are scriptural, my next best are ecclesiastical.

I get so absorbed in linguistic studies that I forget my duty to God and to my fellow-men. I need to be awakened from moral slumber by this terrible doubt as to the state of my own soul.

My great temptation is to the inordinate study of language, as if I would learn all the languages under the sun, and fit myself to be an interpreter at the Tower of Babel.

LAW

Law is the declared will of one in authority.

God's law is not merely the expression of God's arbitrary will; it is the expression of his moral perfections.

God's law is moral law . . . founded on the will of God, but having a ground in the nature of God.

A perfect law of liberty can be found only under a perfect sovereign with a perfect law – that is, God alone.

The first foundation of the amiableness of the law is the character of God.

There is no such thing as a 'law' of nature, except in a figurative sense. The laws of nature do not lead me beyond my own generalizing mind, but moral law does; for if there be not another above me, my Lawgiver, then there is no law for me. You see, I wish to get beneath the voice of my nature to the Maker of my constitution.

We speak of the moral law; we call it law . . . because of the authority that is in it; it is moral, because of this perfection of divine holiness.

We have God, holy, just and good; we have man, made in the image of God, holy, just and good; and between God and man we have a law that man continue to be and act as holy, just and good.

The law is suited, fitted, to make the observer of it happy.

God will multiply to pardon; but modify and take down his law, never.

In every one of the commandments, there is its peculiar beauty.

The end of punishment is not . . . primarily to reform the punished, but to vindicate the law.

Lawlessness is slavery; Christ says so (*John* 8:34).

Its Content

What is the law? Surely a very reasonable one: Be like God.

The law of God is one – multitudes of commandments, but one in its principle; its principle being love to God, and love to all created beings for God's sake.

God could not put aside the law of love, because God is love . . . But what is law? The demand of love.

Law is divided into three parts; legislative, judicial,

executive. Divine differs from human law in that all the functions of government are exercised by God himself.

God's law being exceeding broad affords occupation enough for a man all his life long.

God's law – to superficial minds, to thoughtless minds – is a thing easily exhausted.

Basis of Ethics

Ethics without law is as bad in theology as law without ethics.

God's law is to be studied, that God's will may be done.

Bare ethic, without law, is the ethic of Jehovah alone . . . But whenever subjects appear beneath the sovereign, obligation enters.

Basis of Christianity

The Christian religion is a fact which implies an antecedent ethic. It is without form, and void of meaning, if you do not recognise a preliminary moral law.

Law and Conviction of Sin

By the law the sinner is convinced of a total depravity and an infinite guilt.

It's a serious matter to be under law and to be at the bar and to feel the solemn rigour of jurisprudence.

The question which suggests itself to a man awakened to

see himself described by the law of God is: Can there be a salvation which answers the demands of the law?

Law and Gospel

The law ordained, 'Thou shalt love', and love ordained that law. Man could not keep it; and love ordained a gospel. That gospel is, 'God so loved'. Thus, 'Thou shalt love' is the whole of the law; 'God so loved' is the whole of the gospel.

The law can only be a law of liberty in connection with the gospel.

To each believer the gospel converts the unchanged moral law of God into a perfect law of liberty.

God connected his lawgiving with his liberation – with his salvation (*Exod.* 20:2) . . . Our Liberator is our Lawgiver.

Law is the foundation of duty . . . grace leads to the discharge of it.

Its Effects After Conviction

The Spirit of God, enlightening the convinced sinner, shows him that the precept of the law being holy, just and good, the sanction of the law is holy, just and good too.

When thou art brought to the Mediator, and art down in the dust with closed mouth, what will God do with thee? He will write on thee . . . Surely he will write something good. Yes, his holy, just and good law.

Shorter Sayings

Exhortations regarding the Law

That we may love the law, let us meditate on the law.

While making our meditation on the law, let our hearts burn with love.

Contemplate the law in Christ, the Law-Giver, the Law-Fulfiller and the Law-Exhibitor.

The Legal and the Legalistic

I distinguish between legal and legalistic. It is good to be legal – the gospel is very legal: 'Do we then make void the law through faith? God forbid; yea, we establish the law.'

Legalism and Antinomianism rise from a common root of error.

LIFE

Our life, our death, are not in our own hands; they are in the hands of the Lord.

We are on a solemn journey at all times; and the direction we are taking is of greater consequence than the point we have reached, for our journey is an endless one.

There are interests of Christ's which can be best promoted by our life; there are interests of his which can be best promoted by our death.

He to whom we live, to whom we die, is our Lord.

We are not the world's, not Satan's, not our own; we are the Lord's.

Life is not ours, nor we its; death is not ours, nor we its: we are Christ's, and he is ours.

No Christian should live to himself or die to himself.

Our concerns, Christ's concerns, and Christ's concerns, our concerns.

Oh, is not the life bought by the death of the Lord of glory a good life? a good life for thee, a good life to spend for him?

Oh, what a life of sins and mercies, and then of sins after mercies, and the sins prevent the kindly remembrance of the mercies!

LORD'S DAY

Never since our Lord honoured this day by his resurrection, do I believe has the day passed without some absolute gain to his kingdom.

LORD'S SUPPER

The great connecting link between the first and second coming of the Lord.

All heaven is busy with the work we are about – the commemoration of the death of Christ.

This day, hearing his word and sitting at the table, we are witnessing the fidelity of God to Christ in this promise: 'I will make thy name to be remembered to all generations.'

This feast . . . is the feast of espousals, not that of the consummated marriage.

Jesus is the head of this table.

His love is to his friends at his table, though it was to his enemies when he died.

He who gave himself for you gives himself to you.

The symbols are nothing unless we see Jesus.

It's Christ in the Supper that makes the Supper glorious.

Truth of grace being presupposed, defect of grace is that which this ordinance is designed to meet.

A believer may be an unworthy communicant.

A child may have faith, but he cannot come to the Lord's table, because he cannot examine himself, as an adult can.

'Take, eat' – costly bought, freely given.

Temptation will come after the Supper – it came to Judas, and it came to Peter.

The Lord's table is not ours. We of a particular sect may fence it round, but we have a duty to the church catholic in respect of intercommunion with our brethren. We must not be schismatical, any more than we may be heretical.

To a sobbing communicant: It's for a sinner.

To Moody Stuart after a Communion: Your consecration prayer was not sacramental enough for me.

LOVE

Relation to God, the Supreme, is at the ground of all love.

Love is a self-renouncing, not a self-exalting principle – a self-denying, not a self-aggrandizing principle.

It is lust that is self-aggrandizing, not love.

Even love may be provoked . . . But it takes much, very much, to provoke love; it is not easily provoked.

Love hath to endure; it must, with very much to try it.

God is love, and love suffers long, and is kind.

Love – the greatest of all the graces, greater than faith, greater than hope.

The unloving heart is a suspicious heart, and the loving heart an unsuspicious one.

All true love is founded on proper perception of excellence.

Individual love, *per se*, is a centrifugal force; universal, cosmopolitan love, *per se*, is centripetal; combine them, and the revolutions of love are orderly.

Heaven is the place of perfected love; eternity its duration . . . Have you this love?

In Relation to Law and Gospel

Love is the great attraction. Without the sternness of holiness and justice it would be the love of an unholy and unjust God; yet the holiness and justice of God repel the sinner.

As love is the summary of the law, so it is of the gospel. The law is God's authoritative will that we should love – the gospel is the declaration of God himself loving.

All God's law is, 'Thou shalt love', and all his gospel is, 'God so loved'.

Love is the bond of unity. And what is the law? Just the authoritative demand of the inward bond.

What a noble grace is love! God is love. What says he in the law? 'Thou shalt love'. What says he in the gospel? 'God so loved'.

Love to God

So high a grace requires a worthy object – where shall it be found? Jehovah God claims it to himself.

Our love is in the Scripture set forth, in respect to God the Father, as filial, and in respect to our Lord Jesus Christ, as conjugal.

That command, 'Thou shalt love', has gone down even to hell . . . The obligation of the lost to love him who made them is not cancelled by their unwillingness to render it.

Possess what you may, if you have not love you are nothing, and are getting nothing.

Love to the Lord Jesus Christ

The co-equal, co-eternal Son of God is an adequate object to his Father's love.

Why do believers love Jesus? We cannot answer this question in full, for we cannot describe him in full.

Love to Others

Every creature of God is good, and is to be loved.

Love, love, love, love, the fulfilling of the law.

Love men, love sinners; not their sin, but sinners.

To love a man and to love his sin is to love a man and to love . . . his fever.

I cannot love a man and love his sin.

The unloving heart imagines a hundred evils to be in one's neighbour which don't exist.

My neighbour's good is my good, my Christian brother's spiritual good is my good.

Nothing tends more to promote this principle of love than the cultivation of social religion, and nothing tends more to impede it than the contrary.

Does need or love draw most? I think need, though at the bottom of it you generally find a grain or two of love.

My neighbour's good is my good . . . love makes it so.

It is duty in me to love myself, for it is the measure of the duty I owe to my neighbour, to love him as myself.

MAN

Oh, what a solemn thing it is to be a man! Made so exalted, fallen so low, capable of being raised again so high.

What is man? . . . Man is God's image on earth.

God made man good, but it was a good that was capable of a betterness.

God made man a social being.

We should remember we were in Adam standing before we were in Adam fallen; creation was before the Fall.

We must always remember that man was created before he fell. It is good to take a walk in Eden.

I believe man was made in the image of God, and that he still retains part of that image, it being indestructible.

If we are 'made in the image of God', we can reach and positively apprehend him in whose image we are made.

In Eden, I suppose, there would be the closest sense of intimacy with the greatest sense of distance.

The human mind was not created for independence; God did not make us to be as gods.

Let us not neglect the body; it was created before the soul, and it was assumed by Christ.

Theologically, there are only two men, Adam and Christ.

We are all one race in unity of nature and unity of privilege and of covenant.

God has bound mankind together in his economy of nature, and bound the church together in his economy of grace.

By the Fall

It was the abuse of our freedom that led to the Fall. But it is not absolute pravity, but depravity, that resulted.

Everything is wrong in a wicked man.

I am thinking with horror of the carnal mind, enmity against God. I never get a sight of it but it produces horror, even bodily sickness. Oh, to think that the best man has hatred of God in him!

Man's transgression or departure from the living God neither did nor could lessen his obligations.

If we should say, when man has apostatized, that God should demand less, then man has but to apostatize further, and the claim should be lessened.

When man went away, it was not incumbent upon God to come seeking him.

Man hath gone away from God. God hath come to bring him back. But will fallen man go back?

Man is of noble descent, though he has become of ignoble character.

Our God is lost, Christ lost, the Holy Spirit lost, our happiness is lost, our grace lost, our glory lost, our heaven lost, our souls lost, our bodies lost, our Sabbaths lost, our Bibles lost, ourselves lost, all lost.

If God calls you lost, you must consider yourself lost.

Man is a ruin, but he is a noble ruin.

Let the natural man do his utmost, he is just a well-washed sow.

Man cannot be indifferent – either evil or good, either unholiness or holiness, either pollution . . . or sanctification.

Every man would reproduce himself, and so change God's beautiful diversity into a hideous uniformity.

Man on earth must have a yoke and burden – he cannot find rest without.

If there were a spark of gold in fallen man, it would have come out, it would all gather and cluster round him [Christ].

Oh, what a contrast between human nature in the throne and human nature lying drunk in a ditch!

Do you think of your pravity, and not your depravity? Do you just think of your badness without thinking that you fell out of a good state? You should take a walk in Eden sometimes.

'I am carnal, sold under sin' (*Rom.* 7:14). These words describe what fallen man is, but it is the language of a renewed man.

By Grace

We are all united, both in our degeneracy through one man and in our recovery through another.

A man was our first covenant-head, and a man is our second covenant-head. With no more than two did God ever deal directly – with Adam and with Christ – with all other men mediately through a covenant-head.

Men should be living like dethroned princes; that is but half the truth. Believers should be living like restored princes.

Man's Chief End

All should glorify God, but all will not: in the church alone will God get glory.

God gives, not to end by enriching us – that's an immediate end; but the ultimate end is that he may be glorified.

The cultivation of the human faculties is not man's chief end.

Man's Body

Every man's body is either a temple of the Holy Spirit or of Satan.

MARRIAGE AND DIVORCE

God saw everything that it was good, but that, as far as man was concerned, it was capable of betterness, for the Lord God said, 'It is not good for the man that he should be alone.'

Ill-assorted marriages are forbidden by the Word of God.

Divorce is always a sin against him who made man and woman one pair; but it was not always made theocratic sin, for the law was so regulated as to prevent the rise of unbridled divorce.

MEANS OF GRACE

We make far too little of the means of grace; they are not grace, but they are . . . the middle things of grace, and that is much to us.

See that you despise not what he may in his mercy send; for his blessing can make inferior means not only equally, but more abundantly efficacious.

I had yesterday a pleasant general frame from the ordinance [that is, the Lord's Supper] – an aroma from the gospel field.

We are to assemble to hear God's Word – but to what end? To do it.

MERIT

Merit is the relation between obedience and reward.

Merit is not necessarily annexed to obedience. Merit exists only where there is inherent good. Now there is no inherent good in the volitions of any creature, but only in the volitions of God.

I distinguish merit from praiseworthiness.

MINISTERS AND MINISTRY

The ministry of the gospel is the highest work in which a creature can be engaged.

To 'serve God in the gospel of his Son' is the most honourable and blessed work to which a creature can be called.

The ministry is God's own institution.

The possession of saving grace ordinarily does not complete a man for the work of the ministry.

If God gives the call, he will make us sufficient.

We shall never be ministers unless we get . . . the unction from the Holy One. No teaching of a professor can make up for that. Christ was the greatest of professors, and yet his students needed it. Much more we.

Ministerial Training

The School of Divinity is profitable to those only who have been first taught in another school – the school referred to by Isaiah when he says, 'All thy children shall be taught of the Lord.'

Reverence in the student [that is, of Scripture] is the response to the divine majesty of the Speaker.

Ephesians 4:11,12: I am clearly of opinion that the *didaskalos* [teacher] here is the doctor or professor of divinity, as we term it.

To his students at New Year: Many will be wishing you a happy New Year at this time. Gentlemen, I wish you a happy Eternity.

Ordination

It is strange that all Christendom becomes Presbyterian on an ordination day.

Warnings to the Uncalled

There is every probability (though, blessed be God, not a certainty) that the graceless student will become the graceless minister.

What will the judgment-seat be to the graceless minister?

The orthodoxies, preachings and activities of him who is dead are dead orthodoxies, dead preachings and dead activities.

A good counterfeit minister [makes] a good counterfeit Christian congregation.

Many a so-called Christian teacher is no better than a second-rate heathen moralist.

Needs in the Ministry

To those who never read their Hebrew and Greek Testaments: You profess to preach a book you don't read.

We have too long been acting the part of God's apologists, rather than his heralds.

This is a time which greatly needs two kinds of ministers: namely – sound, zealous, active, popular preachers, and accomplished, thoroughly read, reflective theologians.

For a minister: Let me commend to his meditation 2 Corinthians 3–5 to be studied as a connected whole – a minister's manual.

Meditate, meditate, meditate.

A full gospel ministry has need to be a searching one, and a searching ministry has need to have a very free gospel.

Two Kinds of Congregation

The difficulties in the Christian ministry in any way are great – but it is a very different thing to come among a people who all show outward respect and amongst whom there are souls thirsting after the living God, through whose prayers we are aided, and to meet only with contradiction and blasphemy.

MIRACLES AND THE MIRACULOUS

In the case of the miraculous, the senses cannot now aid us, because the age of miracle is past; but testimony is sufficient for me.

The miraculous is a question of fact, not of philosophy; of testimony, not of speculation – and God can testify as well as man.

Miracles of Christ

I believe the miracles; but I believe in the miracles on account of Christ, instead of believing in Christ on account of the miracles.

If you dispense with the miraculous, there is a whole period of History (that of the Jewish nation), and a single transcendent Life (that of Jesus Christ), and one majestic Story (that of Christendom), which you've got to account for without it and you cannot. These three are inexplicable without miracle.

MUSIC IN WORSHIP

Psalms

On the whole, I prefer the Psalms to the paraphrases and hymns.

George Buchanan's Psalms are magnificent; perhaps the finest translations that we have.

Paraphrases

Our Scottish collection of paraphrases is not good as a whole, nor are they bad as a whole. A few men (none of them poets) merely recast the old paraphrastic hymns of Wesley, Watts and Doddridge, and the result is our paraphrase. They are often too classical, too commonplace.

Hymns

Hymnologies are of great use, but we should have a better selection of hymns. We might have portions of Scripture translated into verse besides the Psalms, keeping as faithfully to the original as the Psalms do. But what I would prefer would be the singing of prose.

The two best hymns in Christendom, in my opinion, are the *Te Deum* and the *Veni Creator Spiritus.*

The *Te Deum* is a grand piece of writing, by far the finest fragment of post-apostolic devotion.

I have a great liking for many of Wesley's hymns, but when I read some of them, I ask, 'What's become of your free-will now, friend?'

Some of the hymns composed for children are very fine. For example, that of Jemima Luke's, 'I think when I read that sweet story of old'.

I am more inclined than once I was, to admit the utility of our having a few hymns, for expressing the clearer objective revelation of the great facts of Christ's history and work. But no hymn-book I have seen gives every phase of subjective religion with the fulness, distinctness, and appropriateness of the Psalms.

Anthems

We might have special anthems for all the prose-poetry of Scripture.

MYSTICISM

Mysticism is not altogether false. Mysticism only errs

when it enters into the province of logic, as logic errs when it trespasses on the domain of intuition, to fetter it.

NATURE AND NATURAL BLESSINGS

Wherefore doth God so clothe the grass of the field? Would it not be as useful without so beauteous a dress? In the wilderness, where no man is, what is the use? It blooms and blossoms in God's own eye, himself delights in it.

I sometimes like to climb a hill, and sit down and look around on this beautiful earth, that I may carry away with me as much of it as I can, and may be able afterwards to remember what this world was like.

Let us have a good dinner; our life in this world is drawing to an end; let us enjoy it while it lasts.

While in Hungary: I've got an extraordinary lesson here; I've learned to read the sunsets, God's sunsets.

NON-ESSENTIALS

It's exceedingly foolish, but exceedingly common, for men to put the *adiaphora* (non-essentials) into the place of the *essentiala* (essentials).

It is strange that you so often find good theologians straining at a gnat and swallowing camels.

OBEDIENCE AND DISOBEDIENCE

Let us remember that perfect obedience is God's demand, which he will not take down.

He will not accept imperfect for perfect obedience.

Obedience now cannot atone for the want of obedience in the past.

You have obeyed the truth. You have not only admitted it to be truth, but have admitted that truth as a guiding, directing, practical, imperative principle.

Merit is not necessarily annexed to obedience. Merit exists only where there is inherent good. Now there is no inherent good in the volitions of any creature, but only in the volitions of God.

If man examines why he disobeys, he will find universally that it is from a notion that he will promote his happiness better by disobedience than by obedience.

OLD TESTAMENT SAINTS

Many of the Old Testament saints lived above their dispensation: most Christians live below theirs.

Let us speak tenderly of the faults of the Old Testament saints.

In estimating the character of an Old Testament saint two common faults are to be avoided: (1) The degradation of them. 'Enoch walked with God'; but 'how can two walk together except they be agreed?' Enoch must have been a regenerated, holy, heavenly-minded man. (2) Their undue exaltation. Full-grown developed Christians they certainly were not. The Old Testament is not to be torn from the New, nor *vice versa*. Surely Messiah was better known to the apostles than to the Old Testament believers! They were heirs, but under a hard discipline. The Great Atonement was not yet made. There is a true doctrine of development in the Scriptures.

ORDER

Let us keep things in order: the beginning for the beginning, the middle for the middle, the conclusion for the conclusion [that is, with respect to our creed].

I am deficient in order; it is sinful; we must remember that God is a God of order.

PANTHEISM

Pantheism has a curious natural affinity with man, when he realises his connection with the Universal Life . . . We live within God's omniprescence, and we have come from him.

I was a Spinozist for three years. The One was then the All to me.

In the poets, in Wordsworth, Coleridge and Thomson, you find much Pantheistic language, but no Pantheism.

I doubt if either Deist or Socinian or Mahommedan will be able to cope with the Pantheist . . . I doubt if any but a Trinitarian can do so adequately.

Pantheism will not account for the phenomena of conscience.

Conscience has no speculative warrant in the system of Pantheism . . . And yet I think that the system is an emphatic admission, or rather proclamation, that there is a secret in the universe that belongeth unto God, un-fathomed and fathomless by men.

Sin gives the lie to Pantheism.

Pantheism, though for a time it may fascinate profound and mystic thinkers, is found at length by earnest souls to be but a splendid cheat. In sinning, you feel you have offended Nobody – no Conscious, Personal, Living God.

PEACE

[The] tranquillity which heavenly-mindedness alone can give – a mind set on heaven, on God in heaven, on Christ in heaven.

He who made peace by the blood of his cross comes now and proclaims peace, and he is the peace.

We . . . obtain peace in contemplating the Lamb of God – peace of conscience which flows from beholding God just when justifying the ungodly – and are enabled to cast our ungodliness [on him] . . . with unsuspecting confidence.

PELAGIANISM

What is it that the Pelagian and the semi-Pelagian attribute to subjective grace (grace in the soul of man) distinct from moral suasion that is not enthusiastic – a sort of spiritual galvanism?

They divide the process in a most arbitrary fashion: one half they give to God, the other half to man. But are these two independent? Does the one not permeate and pervade the other? We hold that the process is not halved and separately shared, but united and conjunctly shared. The whole is God's; the whole is also man's.

PERDITION

'They that are far from thee shall perish.' Perdition! What a word! What a thought! What a thing! To be far from God brings it, *is* it.

PERFECTIONISM

I have less quarrel with a man holding the doctrine of perfection, but I would not like to see the man who thinks himself perfect!

There's nobody perfect – that's the believer's bed of thorns; that's the hypocrite's couch of ease.

God's children are not above the need of teaching.

PERSEVERANCE OF THE SAINTS

The creature cannot stand without the divine upholding, and must fall on the withdrawal of that upholding, while the upholding is not a matter of right, but of sovereignty.

We may abuse the perseverance of the saints, but it is a doctrine clearly taught in Scripture. Yet the fear of apostasy is set before believers.

Wait upon the Lord and he will make your way plain.
Hold fast what you have already learned of him, and pray
for more, study for more, and act for more.

PHILOSOPHERS AND THINKERS

Aristotle

Two things I wonder at in Aristotle: the extent of his
acquirements and the exactitude of his writing.

He is by far the compactest and most precise writer we
have, in any literature.

Robert Boyle

Robert Boyle, the father of English chemistry – a prince
among English philosophers, and a humble follower of
Christ.

Thomas Carlyle

Carlyle's earnestness is very touching and noble; but it
seems to me that according to his teaching, if you could
conceive an omnipotent devil, you ought to worship him
as much as Israel's Jehovah.

Carlyle . . . when he keeps to genuine English . . . has
done a great deal to display the capabilities of English
prose. But he often writes sheer gibberish.

John Foster

. . . a very noble man . . . I cannot think his mind a

healthy one; and that essay of his on 'The Aversion of Men of Taste' I dislike excessively.

Johann Wolfgang Goethe

Goethe said once, all the course of providence goes to show that the God of providence is the same as the severe Jehovah of the Hebrews.

Sir William Hamilton

Sir William Hamilton disliked the theology of Maurice. He was an advocate. No lawyer is likely to fall into a sentimentalism about law.

Immanuel Kant

Kant has ventured on some false correlatives. As sin implies demerit, virtue he thinks implies merit. Kant's correlative is my disparate . . . Kant omits the fact that we are in a state of forfeiture of good, and deserve evil.

Gotthold Lessing

I fear I may not understand Lessing aright; but if I do, that saying of his, which is so much praised – 'Did the Almighty, holding in his right hand *truth*, and in his left, *search after truth*, deign to proffer me the one, I might prefer, in all humility, *search after truth*' – contains the essence of all devilry. It may amount to the willingness to be eternally without God.

J. F. D. Maurice

In Mr. Maurice's system, the ethicist devours the lawyer . . . Maurice's system is pure illegality.

There is no 'should' in his system.

J. D. Morell

That is a very shallow book of Morell's on religion. He may call it the philosophy of religion, but I doubt if it is anything else but cloudification.

Jean-Jacques Rousseau

Rousseau, with his offensive vanity and literary pride, had a curious respect for Christ. With a good bit of the devil in him, he believed and trembled.

The Moral Philosophers

I don't think they have done much more than keep the prison clean, and do effective police work, and that is not an ignoble task. I am not despising one of them.

PHILOSOPHIES

Edwardean: I do not say that the theory of philosophical necessity is innocuous. I believe it is noxious.

Lockean: Locke makes faith to be a matter of probability. But to think that the probability of Jesus being the Christ is as a million of millions to a millionth of a millionth is no degree of faith.

Reidist: I always think that the Reidist conclusion, 'I can't help believing it', is incomplete without some reason in the nature of things . . . Do you not see that without this you are in miserable bondage to a 'can't-help-myself-ism'?

PHILOSOPHY

Baptize philosophy; let her be called Mary, *ancilla Domini* [that is, the handmaid of the Lord]. She may serve but must not rule in Christ's house.

Philosophy was born a pagan, but she may become Christian.

Its Limitations

I cannot reach that by philosophy which God gives by inspiration.

We have been trying to show that God's Word is consistent with the best philosophy. Our business is to 'herald' the good news.

PLEASURE

Unalloyed pleasure is to be found only where there is perfect holiness.

POETRY AND POETS

Much poetry only amounts to rhetorical prose, as much prose is non-versified poetry.

Samuel Taylor Coleridge

To me, when I cannot follow him, there is always a fine ring, like bell-chimes, in his melody . . . I like Coleridge's *Kubla Khan* for its exquisite cadence.

John Milton

Milton's prose is as much worth study as his poetry – sturdy strength, with a grand roll about it.

Alfred Lord Tennyson

Tennyson sometimes comes nearer to Shakespeare than any of our moderns.

William Wordsworth

Wordsworth is very grand at times. He is a better Platonist than many of the philosophers. But I cannot worship nature as he does.

PRAISE
(*see also* MUSIC IN WORSHIP)

It is heaven's work to praise Christ. Let it be earth's work.

PRAYER

We do not speak to a dumb any more than to a deaf God. He is a speaking as well as a hearing God.

As the living God, he is a hearing, speaking God.

God is looking, God is listening, and he will not be mocked by barren sounds.

Fervent prayer moves the hand which moves not the heavens only, but the heart of man.

We little think how much a poor praying woman far off, perhaps at St Kilda, may have to do with the decisions of our General Assemblies.

The Duty of Prayer

If the . . . right to enter in be our privilege, then to enter in is our duty.

The Lord's Prayer

That is God's order in prayer: God first. The believer often puts himself first.

He has taught us to say, 'Thy will be done', and the saying of it will not cost you so much as it cost him.

Posture in Prayer

The most reverential attitude for the worshipper . . . is kneeling at prayer.

Expectancy in Prayer

Prayer is useless if God does not hear; and prayer will be useless to us if, having called, we don't listen that we may get an answer.

Two things make us stinted in prayer – either little feeling of need or little hope of supply.

Two things make us very enlarged in prayer – deep feeling of need and enlarged and strong hope of supply.

Many . . . ask of God earnestly, but not amply: earnestly because they feel need; but not amply, for they think he is a niggard.

I know not whether it be more dishonouring to God to disbelieve that he hears prayer at all, or to think that a little good may be extorted out of an unwilling God.

Get out of your poverty, not by fancying you are rich, but by coming and getting.

Beyond your power to ask and think there lies an infinity of ability to bestow (*Eph.* 3:20).

The prayer 'turn us' is the beginning of turning.

You think he's not willing to give so much: I tell you he's not willing to give so little.

We have far too many preaching prayers; many good ministers preach to God.

Remarks Concerning Himself

I wish you to pray for me that my faith fail not.

Pray for me, pray for pardon, and pray for purity.

There may be some truth at the bottom of what Dr Brown said, 'I think you have more confidence in the prayers of others for you than in the Intercessor'. But I think it is that I have more confidence in their access to him than my own. It may be that I have an impatient desire for assurance.

When I make known my case to my friends, they are more inclined to preach to me than to pray for me.

People would rather preach to me than pray for me; but there is no use preaching to one who is always preaching to himself.

After a lengthy prayer of his own: I fear I have been very long today, but when one thinks he has got in, it is very difficult to get out again.

Other Remarks

I incline to think that prayer should be all in the words of Scripture.

Psalm 85:5: Interrogative pleading, a very powerful form of prayer.

Oh, what reliance shall we put on the intercession of the saints, when Peter and James and John fall asleep?

In whose name do you pray? Not in your own.

The wish to be as God contains within it a prayer for estrangement from God.

How many eyes are toward him whose eye is on us?

A good liturgy forms a fine common bond for the churches.

There is not a right moral relation between Giver and receiver where there is no gratitude.

John 17: Jesus has here a consummating prayer.

'Father, I will.' This is language which is peculiar to Christ. We never read of apostle or prophet so addressing God.

Exhortations to Pray

Don't go and do things innocent in themselves without God's leave. We are servants, and not our own: we must ask leave.

To the unconverted: Pray that you may be made willing to be converted . . . Pray that you may be made very anxious to be converted. Pray that you may be made so anxious as that an unconverted state shall be intolerable to you. Pray that God will teach you what conversion is.

A petition lodged in the name of Christ through the blood . . . is as good as answered.

Prayers of Dr Duncan

O Lord, we are thine; we are thine and wrath is thine; we are thine and salvation is thine; we deserve wrath but we need salvation.

Deepen our humility, enliven our zeal, and inflame our love.

O Lord, I have broken thy law, and I have not believed on thy Son, and I have refused thy Holy Spirit.

When I go to bed I say the child's hymn:

> *This night when I lie down to sleep,*
> *I give my soul to Christ to keep;*
> *If I should die before I wake,*
> *I pray the Lord my soul to take.*

PREACHING

Preaching is the delivery of a message.

The best preaching is: Believe on the Lord Jesus Christ, and keep the Ten Commandments.

The gospel is a light, and when faithfully preached it radiates.

I was a very popular preacher until I began to preach on the work of the Holy Spirit. Then the church grew thin.

I want my religious teacher to give me the nut as it came from God, and to leave it to myself and to God to crack it between us.

It's a striking thing that the whole church likes those who preach experientially to the life of men, apart from the *details* of their doctrine. Yes! the Church's heart beats towards its Lord. Yet I affirm that Calvinistic theology corresponds to catholic experience.

Complaints

There is a sort of preaching in a biblical, orthodox way which sets everybody asleep.

What is our warrant for preaching from texts, or for the excessive amount of doctrinal preaching that abounds? There was little doctrinal preaching till the heresies came.

As heresies exist, doctrinal teaching is a necessity. But we have too much of it in our pulpits. Doctrinal preaching is one thing, doctrinal teaching is another.

There is a possible tendency to put the sermon in place of the true end of preaching.

Balance in Preaching

Some persons preach only doctrine; that makes people all head, which is a monster. Some preach only experience; that makes the people all heart, which is a monster too. Others preach only practice; that makes people all hands and feet, which is likewise a monster. But if you preach doctrine and experience and practice, by the blessing of God, you will have head, and heart, and hands, and feet – a perfect man in Christ Jesus.

Appreciation

I like the clear, shallow men sometimes. Especially I like to listen to their preaching. Even the humdrum theology has its uses.

I like direct practical preaching which helps me to live as a pilgrim on a journey. Now some preach as if they were telling how to make shoes, instead of making them; as if they were describing the process of shoemaking to those who want to be shod. They would have their hearers all taught to be capital shoemakers, while you want to be a shoe-wearer. They tell you all about the leather, and the rosin, and the awl; while it's a rough road for bare feet and cold that you must traverse constantly.

Warnings and Exhortations

Beware of stuffing the text. And yet it is the true excellence of an exposition to see remote connections. The text should not be evacuated.

Beware of him who, if not in matter, yet in manner, preaches himself.

Look for the man who appears most to have seen, most to be beholding the Lamb of God, and whose whole address to you points away from himself and all others to behold the Lamb of God.

PREDESTINATION
(*see also* ELECTION)

Believers are not predestined to be conformed to the image of the unfallen Adam, but to the image of Christ.

PRIDE

Pride does not become a creature. It does not become a

man. It does not become unfallen man . . . How much less does pride become a sinner!

He that glories before God hath not seen God.

All glorying is glorying before God which is not glorying in God.

Sinners are proud.

Holy angels are not proud; fallen angels are; fallen men are; sinners alone are proud beings.

A very usual way for God to bring down the lofty, whether in church or state, is to allow them to dig a pit, and then to fall therein.

You remember that unrecorded saying of the Lord Jesus – unrecorded by any of the four evangelists – 'It is more blessed to give than to receive' – that shows how a poor man can be generous – he can have the generosity of receiving. It is an ungenerous thing, the pride that will not receive.

PROGRESS

Progress is a relative term. It depends on the point from which a man has set out, and on whether he is going up the hill or down it. If I begin from Atheism I have progressed when I become a Pantheist, and I have got a step higher when I am a Theist, though I have a great many steps still to take.

We need a more forward-moving Christianity, with more of the *plerophoria pisteos* [fulness of faith] in it; which is not 'in full assurance of faith', but 'in the full sail of faith', bearing right on with the wind, all canvas up.

There is a destructive school of progress that I cannot endure. It would simply destroy the past to make way for itself.

I do not like to think of railways in the heart of mountains. They are taking them into Greece, and tunnelling Olympus! . . . They'll be watering the engines at Hippocrene!

PROMISES OF GOD

I pray to see in the promises the riches of the Father's love, the value of the Son's obedience, and the mighty power of the Spirit's operation. I must have them or I die.

Most of the gracious promises are in the Old Testament.

The promise of the Spirit is the great comprehensive promise of the gospel.

Ah, to live on the promise we need to live by the Promiser.

Why make a book out of a collection of the promises? Why not as well make a collection of the precepts into a book?

Oh, meditate on the promises. Pray with regard to each promise, 'Good is the mind of Jehovah; be it unto me as thou hast said.' Not one good word shall fail; only believe, hope, wrestle, wait.

PROPERTY AND POSSESSION

There is a difference between property and possession. Though all things are yours, God does not give you all things in possession. That would spoil you.

'All things are yours', but there is one exception: 'Ye are not your own'.

PROTESTANTS

We Protestants are all Dissenters . . . Dissenters from the Church of Rome – Dissenters but not schismatics. Rome was schismatic in forcing us out.

PROVIDENCE

Would we know why the world is governed? It is for the glory of God in his church.

His moral government has a vaster aim than our puny minds can fathom.

It is a blessed thing that we are not placed amid the grinding and wheeling of a great machine of a universe without guiding hand or animating heart.

It seems very religious to dispense with an original creation, in magnifying the ever-present creation of Providence; but it's all a sham. Preservation is not a new creation.

I wonder at the goodness of God, how I have been cared for, provided for – I, a poor shoemaker's son. Providence has been kind.

PSALMS

The Psalms are divisible, else they would be mere rhapsodies, whereas they are unities.

It is a great gift to the church, that Psalter of Israel.

Every emotion of the renewed heart Godwards finds adequate expression in the book of Psalms.

Psalms 1, 2 and 3: Each Psalm has a key-note. That of Psalm 1 is 'Jehovah and his man keeping the Torah'. That of Psalm 2, 'Jehovah and his Anointed'. That of Psalm 3, 'Jehovah's Salvation'.

Psalms 2 & 8: Jesus Christ, the Son of God and the Son of Man, the Son of God of the second Psalm and the Son of Man of the eighth.

Psalm 2: In Psalm 2 we have Christ as the Messiah, the Son of God, the inheritor of all nations . . . we have Jehovah, Jehovah's Anointed, the opposition to Jehovah's Christ, its futility, the blessedness of them that put their trust in the Son of God. The Psalm is wholly Messianic, in no sense Davidic . . . In its form Psalm 2 is dramatic. 1. The Psalmist speaks. 2. Jehovah speaks. 3. Messiah speaks. The Psalmist concludes.

Psalm 3 . . . is a morning Psalm.

Psalm 4: This is an evening Psalm . . . It sings of Jehovah's peace.

Psalm 8: Very likely this Psalm was the first sung by David, and given to his children some night as they were at family reading and singing – for it is evidently a night

Psalm – and when their passage for the night was Genesis chapter 3 . . . In Psalm 8 we have Christ as man, the Son of man, made Lord of all . . . The Jews referred the eighth Psalm to Adam, but it refers to Christ the second Adam. This circumstance is both its veil and its beauty.

Psalm 19: This Psalm consists of two parts: (1) Revelation of God in nature to all; (2) In the Torah, more particularly, to Israel . . . It is a fine thought, the eternal present in nature's praise of God: 'The heavens are declaring' etc. – one day uttering speech to another, and one night teaching its successor.

Psalm 37:7: 'Rest in the Lord.' Not only on, but in the Lord. The soul will not rest long on that which it does not rest in, in which it does not acquiesce.

Psalm 51:2: 'Cleanse me from my sin.' Blessed thought, gentlemen! My sin and I can be separated. No doubt it is *my* sin, but it is not *myself* – not a natural, original, essential part of myself.

Psalm 73: This is a song of deliverance . . . The 73rd Psalm is a minor book of Job – only not carried out so far . . . The great subject of Psalm 73 is his deliverance from the temptation which he had . . . His temptation was as to the goodness and profitableness of godliness . . . Now, we have not a better God than Asaph had, but (thanks to his name) we have a much more fully-revealed God than Asaph had.

Psalm 87: This Psalm is prophetic and Pentecostal.

Psalm 110: In Psalm 110 we have Christ as David's Lord, at God's right hand, till all things are under his feet.

Psalms 127 and 128: These two Psalms form a pair. They seem from internal structure to have been sung by the people coming up at the three great annual festivals.

Psalm 131: This is a song for the Valley of Humiliation. I have been often there.

REDEMPTION

The redemption-price from condemnation is something given unto condemnation, in order that we may not be given unto condemnation.

I am inclined to think that the great end of human redemption is the full manifestation, as of the divine perfections, so of the divine Tri-unity.

Jesus did not come to deliver from anything else than the alienation from God.

You are redeemed from the curse of the law, and so from the law as a covenant of works.

It is not merely the truth, but the justice of our redemption, that conscience has to deal with.

Calculate, calculate, if you can, the value of redemption. It is so precious! What has it cost you? You? Nothing at all. But it cost the Lamb himself!

REGENERATION

That which is born of the flesh is flesh, sinful and mortal; but that which is born of the Spirit is spirit, holy and immortal.

There is not always pain at the new birth of the soul.

Is man active or passive in regeneration? He is both; he is active *about* it and passive *in* it.

In the fallen nature, the elective faculty remains undestroyed . . . and though we are in one sense passive in regeneration, in another sense we are not. We yield our wills up to the active *energeia* [power] of the higher will.

The new life in regeneration . . . is yet but a beginning, and the converted man is like the new-born child.

1 John 3:9: The new creature does not sin, but the complex man, in whom the new and old man is, he sins. These two, while inconsistent and contrary, are not incompatible.

What a work is the work of regeneration: whether we consider him who regenerates or that which is regenerated.

Its Necessity

If it were possible to behold Christ without regeneration, it were possible to enter heaven without regeneration.

To a divinity student: Do you believe in the necessity of regeneration? . . . Do you believe it necessary for a minister to be born again to preach the gospel?

Whatever becomes of the heathen, you will be damned yourself unless God save you by the washing of regeneration and renewing of the Holy Ghost.

Shorter Sayings

An Encouragement

As good earth, water and sunshine won't make a dead plant grow, so Bibles, good churches and ministers won't cure spiritual death. Is the cause hopeless then? No, for 'God quickeneth the dead'.

REGULATIVE PRINCIPLE

While Luther put away all that he could prove from the Bible to be manifestly false, Calvin would admit only what the Bible showed to be true. 'Nothing anti-biblical', says Luther; 'Nothing unbiblical', says Calvin.

RELIGION

The nature of all true religion . . . is love to God for what God himself is.

In the infinite and perfect amiableness of God, we have the foundation of all religion.

Subjective religion is just intensely objective religion.

The Old Testament religion is not mere monotheism – it is Jehovism.

True religion does not make angels and glorified saints miserable; true religion did not make Adam and Eve miserable. But true religion here is in sinners, and so there may be something of that in them. However, it is not religion that makes them miserable, but the want of it.

Aesthetic Religion – The Worship of the Beautiful

A merely aesthetic religion . . . is the offspring of sentiment divorced from law.

Aesthetic religion is at bottom the bringing of religion to God instead of bringing the soul to God to get religion.

Sin and Death . . . cast two shadows over man in this life which give the lie to a religion merely of the beautiful.

There is no entering into the kingdom of heaven by a mere sense of beauty.

Aesthetical religion seems always disposed to kick at the curse of the law, and the theologians in whom the sentimental has extinguished the jurisprudential have not fully understood the nature of sin.

Warnings About Religion

Beware of religion without God.

You do no good by changing the vocabulary of religion. If you change the words, you change the thoughts.

Let the effort to clothe yourself with the raiment of the beautiful be changed into an effort to strip yourself.

I have not much sympathy with those who have great suspiciousness about false religion. I have not much sympathy with strong, positive [condemnatory] affirmations about people's religion, where there is nothing decidedly bad. I have not much sympathy with those who are not disposed to admit and to hope that there may be reality, where there is the appearance of some little good thing towards the Lord God of Israel.

Every one should have a strait creed for himself, and a wide one for other people.

REPENTANCE

Adam stepped away from God into sin, and a sinner who repents turns away from sin unto God.

If we desire some noble employment . . . what better thing can there be than returning to God?

It is good to return from folly to wisdom . . . from vice to virtue . . . from sin to happiness; but it is best of all to return [from sin] to God.

When God says, 'Return', you must return, or you must shut your ears and harden your hearts.

God needs to do a great deal to sinners in order to turn them; but God is requiring nothing of sinners but that they return.

While we are bound to return unto God, God is under no obligation . . . to take us back.

What at every moment is required of the wicked and unrighteous man? To cease being what he is.

Repentance is both a grace and a duty.

Repentance is better than innocence, not absolutely, but in so far as man is concerned.

Sinning is not a rare thing – but repentance is.

The sorrows of genuine repentance are deeper than those caused by legality.

One sinner can make all heaven glad.

Is there no sinner here – no one individual sinner – who would like to make all heaven ring for joy? Repent, repent, repent; and make all heaven shout at the sight.

Has he drawn you from yourself? That requires the most drawing force of any.

Its Necessity

It is . . . not so much that man fell from holiness and happiness as that he fell from God; and it is not so much that he needs to return to holiness and happiness as that he needs to return to God.

It was by turning from God that we turned to sin; and turn as we like, till we turn to God we are godless.

Its Relation to Christ

Jesus died to procure – Jesus rose to confer – repentance and the forgiveness of sins.

Genuine repentance flowing from faith in the crucified Saviour.

Warnings

When men conceive that in being called upon to repent, they are called upon to do anything short of undoing what

Adam did in his disobedience, their repentance is not genuine.

Nothing is more pernicious than light definitions of repentance.

Sinner, you are away from God. And sinner, you can never prosper being away from God.

Sinner, you must go back to God – you must go back to God.

REVELATION

It is the great glory of God's revelation that it has changed our abstracts into concretes: the infinite existence into the I AM of the Old Testament, the personal Jehovah; the infinite love into the personal Christ.

REVIVAL

There are tides in all things, and the greatest wave of divine blessing seems to keep ebbing and flowing amongst the churches.

The church, as it has advanced in time, has advanced in wisdom, but, oh, what a declension in fervour!

The revivals, as Dr Cunningham said, may leave some thousands converted.

A conversation with Dr Duncan: 'We are not thirsty yet', he said in speaking of prayer for the Holy Spirit. 'How do you know?' 'Because it is written, "I will pour water upon him that is thirsty", and "When the poor and needy seek water, and there is none, and their tongue faileth for thirst, I the Lord will hear them, I the God of Jacob will not forsake them". If our tongue were failing for thirst, we should have the water. We live under the Pentecostal economy of the Holy Ghost; what was done that day was but the opening scene. It was a splendid opening no doubt, but it was the splendid entering in of a perpetuity.'

On an occasion when the Presbytery had recommended ministers to preach specially on the work of the Spirit: I doubt the wisdom of the proposal. I think that no extensive awakening has ever been produced by preaching on the work of the Spirit, but rather by awakening the conscience and setting forth Christ.

ROMAN CATHOLICISM

No doubt many a devout soul has found its spiritual nourishment in that church. Wheat and arsenic, wheat and arsenic; it all depends on the proportions.

There are magnificent prayers in the Missal. They are chiefly relics of a very early and much purer age; and many a good Romanist gets on very well in his church by the help of these alone.

You will never find a Roman priest wandering from the catholic faith on the Person of Christ, or in reference to the Trinity.

The Romish devotee is wrong only in going to the wrong priest.

SALVATION

It is as yet an unseen but not an unannounced salvation (*1 Pet.* 1:5).

The salvation of God in its essence is the same in all ages . . . But the Old and New dispensations are very different.

The scheme of salvation is entirely supernatural.

There is a strong sense of justice in a man; he will not consent to condemnation unless he sees that it is just; and he will not consent to be saved unless he sees that it is just through grace; it must be just grace. Law and grace are wonderful things.

Oh, the magnitude of that great salvation of God! My feeble faculties can never cope with it.

We all naturally, in our fallen state, have a feeling of revulsion at the thought of a scheme of a salvation that gives man no occasion for boasting or vain-glory.

If there were universal salvation, there would be universal repentance.

The human race: In the state of condemned criminals under the king's reprieve – allowed, it is true, the best of prison fare.

Men cannot be saved without atonement and without regeneration.

A human righteousness answering all the demands of the law must be found if we are to be saved.

Christ came to save the contrasts of himself, but not to leave them such.

Christ came to save the contrasts of himself. He has come with wisdom for the foolish, with righteousness for the unrighteous, with sanctification for the unholy, with redemption for the ruined.

By Grace

That salvation is entirely of grace is equally plain, not only to exegesis, but also to the feeling of everyone who by the teaching of the Holy Ghost has discovered himself to be lost, entirely lost.

He will damn you whatever you do, unless he save you of mere grace – there is no other way for you or me.

Salvation is of grace, but it is of grace which makes good workers.

Ephesians 2:9, 10: 'Not of works' – otherwise it were no salvation *for sinners*; 'Unto' or 'For good works' – otherwise it were not a *salvation* of sinners.

Its Experiential Aspect and Order

The principal thing God does for us is what he does in us.

As in the life of the Lord Jesus . . . there were steps . . . of humiliation, so also salvation . . . comes out in steps: in salvation by grace from the power and guilt of sin; then, for the soul at death, from the inbeing of sin; and finally, for the soul and body at the resurrection . . . from death and all the penal effects of sin.

First, Christ apprehends us; second, we receive him, third, we give ourselves to him; fourth, we give ours, both the dispensed and the retained, to him.

Exhortations

If any of you are concerned about your soul's salvation, do not delay, but come to Christ at once.

We cannot save your souls, friends. All the ministers in the world, taken together, could not. We cannot save our own . . . Behold the Lamb of God.

SANCTIFICATION

Purifying work is sorrowful work: sorrow at the thought of being impure, yet joy at the thought of coming purity.

You see how intimately our justification and our sanctification are connected; and our justification, when we apprehend it deeply enough, is the virtual execution of our sins. It is the sentence of God to slay our sins, and to save our persons. and here we stand between two ultras. It is the evil extreme of Romanism, that it deprives sanctification of its legal grounds; and it is the evil of an ultra-Protestantism that it stops short at the act of justification, or omits the very close nexus between it and sanctification.

SANDEMANIANISM[1]

The secret of Sandemanianism is this: it is the doctrine of justifying righteousness along with the Popish doctrine of faith ... The story is told of a man who was seeking admission somewhere to church fellowship, who, on being asked, 'Do you believe the faithful saying that Christ Jesus came into the world to save sinners?' answered, 'It's a glorious truth, whether I believe it or not!' That answer would have delighted Sandeman.

SATAN

It is a strange thing that so fine a spirit is let loose to do so much mischief.

He is but a creature, and cannot know the secrets of the universe.

I believe I would be morally bound for ever to adore the justice that banished me. And I would not deny that hopeless love is still the devil's duty.

I suppose Satan will retain still the feeling of having been an unfallen angel once; he cannot get quit of his angelicism.

In reply to the question, 'Can the tempting of Satan be distinguished from the seduction of sin?': Oh, yes; I've caught him at it.

---

[1]Robert Sandeman (1718–71) whose teaching was believed to reduce saving faith to mere intellectual assent.

1 John 2:12–13: The believer passes from the state of childhood to that of youth when he gains his first victory over Satan.

Exhortation

There is One to whom thou didst belong before thou didst belong to Satan. Creation was before the Fall . . . Thy true Master and Lord calleth thee: Come away, come away from the kingdom of Satan into the kingdom of God's dear Son.

SCIENCE

In the nature of things it is impossible that science can ever discover the existence of God, because science deals with phenomena . . . but God is not a phenomenon.

There is a fine analogy between science and theology. A world is made, and science is incipient. A revelation is made, and theology is incipient. You quarry facts, and place them, cut and polished, in the temple of science; and you gather other facts, and build them into the temple of systematic theology.

SELF-EXAMINATION

Whoever discourages self-examination makes void the First Epistle of John.

It is good to lay stress upon self-examination, but don't make too little of believing; find 'all joy and peace in believing', in very believing.

SELF-EXPRESSION

The summons to let your nature, whatever it may be, get free play, with all its corrupted instincts, is a summons to pandemonium.

SELF-FULFILMENT

'Fulfil yourself' is the vague and cloudy cry of some shallow analysts of man's nature. Fulfil what? . . . Your fallen nature, or the new creature?

SELF-SUFFICIENCY

There is no presumption I know of so great as that which fancies sufficiency for what an apostle found himself insufficient (*2 Cor.* 3:5, 6).

SIN

The only solution of sin and misery compatible with God's benignity and holiness is the Fall.

It is not, 'The cruel God loves misery', but, 'The righteous God loves righteousness.'

God is the author of all entitive acts, but he is not the author of sin.

The permission of sin is adorable, the actual fact of sin is abominable [quoting Samuel Rutherford].

The whole might of Godhead is opposed to iniquity.

A lie brought all sin into the world.

God is the source of every free as well as every determined act, but he is not the cause of the evil that is in acts, whether free or determined.

Our finite sin cannot be urged against his infinite mercy.

The Nature of Sin

Sin is a monstrous, unnatural, miserable thing.

Sin is an off-cutting, a degeneracy, a cancer or corruption consequent on privation.

As darkness is the privation of light, and death the absence of life, sin is the privation of good.

Sin is first privative, and then positive.

Evil is a fact, but not an entity. It is not a 'thing' at all. It is a minus quality.

Sin is spiritual nakedness.

In a theocracy God is king and sin is crime. Sin, which is made crime by the theocratic law, is both sin and crime. It is sin as against the Lord of the whole earth, and crime as against the king.

Sin is bondage, the bondage of corruption.

Sin and death are monstrous anomalies. It was never intended that we should either die or sin.

God has made human nature a fine nature. Sin is something monstrous, both to devils and men, and so is self-punishing.

Sin . . . not only deserves wrath, but is in itself enmity.

Sin is the infinitely horrible, the curse is the infinitely terrible, and salvation from that horrible is not enough without salvation from that terrible, while deliverance from that terrible is impossible without salvation from that horrible.

All sin designs deicide.

All transgression is ambitious, and if it could succeed it would scale the universe and dethrone its monarch.

Sin . . . is a cancer, which, if it could spread itself unchecked, would eat up all being, and dethrone God himself.

The Root of Sin

It is distrust of Jehovah's goodness that lies at the root of transgression . . . man ceases to depend upon God for good, and then, depending upon himself, he seeks happiness by transgression.

The desire to ensure self-happiness, and independence, and private good, is the root of sin.

The Consequences of Sin

The wages of sin is death, and till that is paid, there is no getting near to the God that I have offended.

Sin stains the conscience.

God punishes sin with sin: 'You dishonour me by idolatry, I give you up to dishonour yourselves.'

Sin has brought not simple disorganisation but perdition into our universe – perdition into our souls, perdition into all our services.

Sin has vitiated the course of nature, the course of rational and moral nature as well as of physical nature.

The Guilt and Punishment of Sin

The guilt of sin is the product of two things: first, of sin which is the transgression of the law; and second, of justice which is the maintenance of the law.

Every sin will be adequately punished; blessed be God, not every sinner.

All sin is damning in its nature.

Guilt is the relation between disobedience and punishment. Transgression and justice produce guilt.

It is a righteous thing in God to mark iniquity.

Now if all sin was visited with death . . . no flesh could live; so holy is God, so sinful is man.

Indwelling Sin

I defy man or angel to free themselves from guilt without an atonement, and to free themselves from depravity without regeneration.

Sin that dwelleth in me – Oh, to think of having that hellish thing in us as long as we live!

Will the carnal mind lie down and submit to be slaughtered like a lamb? No, it will resist to the very last; it will only yield when grace has conquered it.

While all within is evil, nothing external can rectify it.

Between sin and grace there is waged in the believing soul a war interminable, till, through the strength of the Captain of salvation, the whole body of sin and death be abolished, and the glorified soul be satisfied with Christ's likeness, seeing him as he is.

Although there is grace in your heart, there is also corruption, both wishing the mastery.

A saint, when overborne by indwelling sin, ought to comfort himself with the thought that a prisoner of war is not a deserter.

The flesh cannot do what it would, for the spirit will not let it; and the spirit cannot do what it would, for the flesh will not let it.

Committing Actual Sin

If one sin destroyed man's moral nature, every sin strengthens man's depravity.

Guile, deceit, falsehood, is a cloak which men wrap over their sin.

I have never been a day but I have been sinning.

Acting according to the corruption of nature is mistaken by man for acting according to nature; . . . and to act according to nature is to be free – hence man thinks sin freedom.

A man should not do wrong for gain's sake. A man should prefer eternal right to everything else.

What's a world's sin? The sin of a race that for six thousand years has been sinning? What the amount of actual sin? What then the depravity of nature, which is the well-spring of it all?

Had we but a sight of Glasgow's sin for one day – Oh, what a terrible sight it would be! All Glasgow would be struck with horror!

A half-truth generally ripens into a manifest lie.

By riotous living we are to understand all enjoyment that is not of God.

Ah! sin is easily committed . . . but . . . it is not easily confessed.

The Expiation of Sin

To expiate sin can be nothing else than the full endurance of that which sin deserves.

A True Sense of Sin

Though every man acknowledges himself a sinner, we have naturally little idea of what sin means.

Ah! we can form little conception of sinlessness!

The unregenerate man thinks that sin is liberty, but not so the man taught of God.

None can know sin without the knowledge of the law, and none can know the law without the knowledge of God and his perfections.

It's great forgiveness he bestows, and he'll have us know this by setting the greatness of our sins before us.

Oh, how bitter are the fruits of sin, and when they are felt how sweet the consolations of God!

You don't know how I have sinned; there's no good in polluting my lips by confessing it to man.

I have never done a sinless action during the seventy years. I don't say but by God's grace there may have been some holy action done, but never a sinless action.

To me belongeth shame and confusion of face, and so I will take it.

Confessing Sin

Oh, how sweet it is to confess sin before a sin-forgiving God! a sin-forgiving God!

The Lord give us open hearts, to hide no sin from him, that, while we confess with shame, we be not ashamed to confess!

It is an act of grace to deliver the self-confessed sinner . . . The confessing and forsaking of sin are no atonement for sin.

Confessing to those we have offended: The mind is so constituted that without confession it cannot be at peace . . . A man . . . can never be fully assured of his willingness to confess till he has made confession.

Pardon or Forgiveness of Sin

Though he will multiply to pardon, he will not change the law.

Pardon restores violated relations. Whoso receiveth pardon as pardon, desireth to stand in the peace of God.

It is magnanimity in God to forgive sins.

The faith that receives pardon (not bare impunity) cannot but be penitent, for it receives the peace of God. You do not ask your friend's pardon unless you mean to be friends with him. A child does not ask his father's pardon if he means to quit the house.

There are no indulgences; sins are forgiven, but they are never treated as debts.

Psalm 51:3: Pardoned sin ought to be before us. God says in the covenant concerning our sins, 'I will remember them no more', but 'Then shalt thou remember and be confounded, and never open thy mouth any more because of thy shame.'

Oh, my soul, how much thou owest! Ten thousand

talents. 'When they had nothing to pay, he frankly forgave them.' 'Much hath been forgiven her – she loved much.' O my soul, what is thy desire? The great forgiveness and the great love.

Oh, my soul, let the forgiveness enter thy conscience; it will introduce the love into thy heart.

We have never done one act that did not need to be pardoned.

The . . . original transference of our sin, if we would see it, is not either in the day of our pardon or in the day of atonement, but in the day of the everlasting covenant.

Pardon under the Old Testament: God pardoned the sin under the Old Testament on the credit of Christ's death.

Warnings Against Sin

Be still, and before you oppose God in his legislation or in his grace, be still, and count the cost.

Don't make use of past evidences of grace against present charges of sin.

Don't think that because sin is merely privative, it is less horrible than if it were positive, or less terrible in its consequences.

Know you how hard a thing it is first for an unsaved sinner to believe that God is so strict in his justice, and then for a convinced sinner that God is so rich in his mercy?

Regarding its deceitfulness: Sin says, 'I'm pleasant'. Yes, pleasant poison.

Prayers and Exhortations Regarding Sin

Oh, that he would break our hearts for sin and from sin!

Oh, for such a look of Christ as will scatter sin.

If the guilt of sin oppress you, oppose to it that Jesus Christ who died is God; and if the power of sin oppress, oppose to it that the Holy Ghost who sanctifies is God.

It's best not to fall, but if you fall be sure to rise again.

So let us not set our sin above the forgiveness which is with God.

Blessed thought: my sin and I can be separated.

SINCERITY

'He's at least sincere' is a common saying . . . Of course, that is something . . . I doubt not that the present Pope is a very sincere papist, and I believe that Torquemada was a very sincere inquisitor!

But that he has acted conscientiously does not prove that a man has done his duty . . . Sincerity is not . . . the equivalent of duty.

SINGING IN WORSHIP

Standing when singing is the best attitude. Musical men say it is the best posture for the voice, and I say it is the most reverential attitude for the worshipper.

I believe some of the good people think good singing in parts a sin – also to sing in any way but very slowly. The

drawling singing came in in the days of Moderatism. We
have degenerated from former times.

SPECULATION

I got no rest to the sole of my foot till I rejected all
speculation.

When I gave up my sceptical opinions I did not pick them
out one by one, but I got a vomit, and vomited them all
up . . . and admitted the Bible just at once.

I have speculated a great deal during my life, but now that
I am turning into an old man, I am in love with the facts.

SPIRITUAL FRAMES AND CONDITIONS

At their best moments, regenerated men are never so good
as to be without sin; at their worst, they are never so bad as
to be entirely destitute of good.

Complaining of our spiritual wants to our fellows should
be at least sparingly and wisely done. We profess to
belong to a rich and bountiful Master; and our complaints
lead, almost force, men to think either that we are
hypocrites or that he is not such as we declare him to be.

Galatians 5:17: In the complex man there is a two-fold
will – to do good, and to do evil. The intention of the flesh
is the total destruction of the spirit, and the intention of
the spirit is the total destruction of the flesh; and the war is
internecine.

One of Dr Duncan's experiences: It is not a clean desertion. It is very dirty. The great Physician best knows the symptoms of my malady, but I know the cause: a life of self-pleasing instead of to the glory of God – backsliding. And now, when there is the desire to return, there comes the difficulty. Oh, I have need of the hospital. 'Heal my soul, for I have sinned against thee' (*Psa.* 41:4).

Beware of backsliding. It greatly grieves the Holy Ghost, provokes God, and brings forth the bitterest fruit (*Prov.* 14:14).

The Lord turns the darkness into light; and it is not merely that he brings light after the darkness, but the darkness itself he makes into light.

Enjoy the honeymoon as long as you can, but be not astonished if days of darkness should come.

It is a trying time for a man when he has been seven years converted . . . he is out of his first straits, and he has got most of his questions answered; he stops inquiring, and is apt to settle on his lees and get into darkness.

Many a time a child of God walks in darkness, not because he is blind, but because it is night with him.

The balm of Gilead must be applied by the Physician there.

True discoveries humble a man.

The Lord's people are a singing people, and their way is a singing way. But also the Lord's people are a weeping people, and their way is a weeping way.

There is sorrow, not in the service, but for having served before, and . . . because the service is so poor and defective. But there is no sorrow in the service.

SUPERNATURAL

I am not conscious of the supernatural. I am only conscious of the natural, of faculties and states. But I know a great deal more . . . than I am conscious of.

I say that the whole character of Hebrew history attests the supernatural, and if you add the two nobler chapters from the book of history – the life of Jesus Christ and the story of the Christian church – destructive criticism has a good deal to account for!

THEOLOGIANS

Augustine and Calvin

Augustine was greater on the whole than Calvin. Calvin is the more complete; no thanks to him for that, for Calvin was standing on Augustine's shoulders, Augustine on his own feet.

Richard Baxter

Richard Baxter lives in the affection of the church, yet he greatly perplexed the gospel; he tried to make peace between the Calvinists and Arminians by getting some middle way.

Baxter was in my eyes a great muddler, but the whole church cannot help liking Baxter for all his muddling.

He was a singularly great man in his power of dealing with the conscience, and he made a revolution in the town of Kidderminster.

Baxter complicates the doctrine of grace in trying to find a middle way. Baxter and Fuller (who is Baxter *minor*) and Howe (more evangelical than either) have laboured well the following sphere, which some good men don't touch. We are passive in our regeneration, but we are not to be passive *about* our regeneration.

Robert Bellarmine

Bellarmine was not the worst kind of papist – far from it; but he always raises a desperate cuttle-fish confusion about him, and then puts out his claw and drags.

J.A. Bengel

Bengel's short *Scholia*[1] are amongst the very best on the New Testament.

Thomas Boston

Boston has great tenderness of conscience, but I think there was a legality and pernicketiness; I think that a great deal of what he called desertion was just low spirits.

---

[1]*Scholia* = comments, the reference being to Bengel's *Gnomon Novi Testamenti* (1742), reprinted in revised form as *The Critical English Testament*, eds. W. L. Blackley and J. Hawes (Strahan & Co.: London, 1869), 3 vols.

There were two things in him: he was looking only to Christ for justifying righteousness, and he was seeking to walk before God in all well-pleasing.

Boston was a commonplace genius; mark, I do not say a commonplace man, but a commonplace genius.

Bradwardine and Twisse

In Bradwardine and Twisse, the lawyer threatens to swallow up the ethicist.

George Buchanan

Buchanan would have got great advancement in the church had he only truckled to them.

W.C. Burns

I was not his spiritual father, but I think I was his nurse.

George Campbell

I got hold of a volume of George Campbell's in which he ridicules the notion that to God there is no past, present or future – to him all are one. I remember well how I abhorred George Campbell for that.

Thomas Chalmers

Ah! my doctrine about faith was better than his, but he went to prayer, and his faith was better than mine.

Chalmers and I had a discussion about faith. I admired the doctor's faith, but not his definition. It was Sandemanian, but rectified by better views of the work of the Spirit.

Chalmers was not a widely read divine, but as a practical thinker and teacher of the heart he was unrivalled.

Chrysostom

Chrysostom, the rhetorical St John.

I do not know what the bishops of the east do now, but John Chrysostom was in his cathedral daily, preaching to crowded audiences.

Though no Pelagian, in his expository ethics he often talks Arminian-like. But his Christology keeps him right.

Adam Clark

Dr Adam Clark is one of the best masters of English prose . . . his style is the most perfect blending of the Saxon and the Latin that I know of.

William Cunningham

In old age: Hercules still, but he has no club.

Franz Delitzsch

I have the highest opinion of Delitzsch as a commentator. He is the finest Jewish Belles-Lettrist existing.

The Early Church Fathers

There is far too little study of these men in this age of superficiality.

Oh, the Fathers, dear men, they were poor theologians, but they were excellent for burning!

Jonathan Edwards

But look at the Edwardean theology, omitting this its metaphysical blot. It was steeped in the affections. That will keep any man safe amid intellectual aberration, and prevent it telling on his life.

In the Edwardean ethics you see a fine moral stoical Christianity in conjunction with the finest affections.

His doctrine is all application and his application is all doctrine.

In Jonathan Edwards and the New Englanders we have a fine union of moral law and moral ethic . . . With all his rigour, Edwards is supremely moral.

Edwards and Boston

I would like to sit at Jonathan Edward's feet, to learn what is true religion, and at Thomas Boston's, to learn how I am to get it.

Between Boston and Edwards there is no contradiction, and they are important to each other.

I would like to see a divine arise in whom Jonathan Edwards and Thomas Boston were thoroughly welded into one.

Erasmus

Poor Erasmus truckled all his life for a hat. If he could only have been made a cardinal! You see the longing for it in his very features!

Thomas Erastus

Poor Erastus! A physician! What did he know about it?

Fenelon and Leighton

I think that both Fenelon and Leighton were men constitutionally afraid of the full blaze of the truth. They were naturally timorous men.

Ferme on Romans

You here see Aristotle and Quintilian combined, working away at St Paul . . . Ferme must have known Ramus, if he did not know Aristotle.

Andrew Fuller

Andrew Fuller – a distinguished Baptist minister, and author of some judicious works.

John Gill

Gill has written the best commentary I know in English on the Gospel of John. He is in it richly trinitarian.

Gill and Crisp were the best theologians among the Antinomians. Gill's edition of Crisp's works . . . contains some excellent matter.

Thomas Halyburton

I advise every theologian to acquaint himself with Halyburton . . . He neither understates nor overstates the value of the law to the gospel, and the necessity of the gospel to the law.

He was naturally a sceptic, but God gave that sceptic great faith. His book against the Deists . . . is a scholastic prosecution of Owenian principle.

Matthew Henry

Matthew Henry is not deep, but broad . . . because he cast himself with equal reverence upon the whole of the Bible, and had no favourite texts.

Thomas à Kempis

A fine fellow, but hazy, and weak betimes. He and his school tend . . . to make humility and humiliation exchange places.

William Law

A mystic, and in his mysticism at times a Christian Pantheist, and strongly opposed to imputation. Yet he spoke as with the sound of a trumpet upon the practical. The mystical and the practical are seldom so united as they were in him.

Spurious spirituality is very dangerous. William Law – his *Serious Call* – what a striking book it is yet it contains the denial of the atonement. William Law seems to me to have been a legalist of a very peculiar type. I have read somewhere that the last words of William Law were these: 'Away, away with the filthy rags. A flame is kindled in my soul that will burn to all eternity in honour of Jesus Christ.'

John Love

I am neither company for a sinner nor a saint, but I think that if Dr Love were alive I could speak to him.

Luther and Melanchthon

If a subject could be split into twelve separate points, and also compressed into one, Luther would take the one, Melanchthon the twelve.

Marrowmen[1]

They did hold that faith has in it objective assurance and appropriation; but their appropriation is not their *believing*

[1] A group of Scottish ministers, among whom were Thomas Boston and Ebenezer and Ralph Erskine, who defended the doctrine contained in a work entitled *The Marrow of Modern Divinity* (1645). The book was condemned by the General Assembly of the Church of Scotland in 1720.

that I have received Christ, but *receiving Christ.* I don't bind myself to the Marrow doctrine; but they were fighting a good fight against Neonomianism [a reaction to Antinomianism which, by its emphasis on good works in the Christian, overshadowed the doctrine of justification by faith alone].

If I met a man from New England, I would say to him, 'Read the Marrowmen!' If I met a Marrowman, I would say to him, 'Read the New England men.' They are the complement of each other.

Duncan Mearns

It was Dr Mearns who satisfied me of the existence of God.

I was much indebted to Dr Mearns . . . It was under him that I gave up atheism.

John Milne

Now, we'll have some sweet Christian experience from John Milne; he keeps his theology right by his experience.

A. Moody Stuart

In soul analysis I would say he is first, and in other things fair; and a man who is first in one thing and fair in others is no common man.

John Muir

That man owes much to divine grace; except for grace Dr Muir would have been a Socinian.

George Müller

It is a strange work, his taking the Sermon on the Mount altogether literally – selling all that he had and giving to the poor. Well, the Lord has blessed it in his case. He has taken it literally and he has prospered.

J. H. Newman

. . . the subtle devout man.

Brownlow North

. . . an untrained theologue . . . a born theologian.

John Owen

John Owen has vigorous thoughts, but the baldest style I know . . . he was a good student of texts. But oh, he moves clumsily. He moves like a whale . . . but . . . he is great in spiritual analysis. He is at the head of a school of divines.

Polycarp

I have often thought that good Polycarp, the disciple of the apostle John, could scarcely have stood a theological examination by Dr Owen; but oh, Polycarp and these men were notable men, to burn for the cause of Christ!

Matthew Poole

Poole's Annotations are well suited to the well-instructed

laity. Henry is too diffuse a commentator for them: he is more for the country people.

Puritans

I believe that the Puritan age had a depth that we know nothing about.

E. B. Pusey

He has a fine spirit of reverence for the Word of God . . . His Christianity radiates back to that of Augustine; he is an Augustinian.

F. W. Robertson of Brighton

Robertson believed that Christ did something or other, which, somehow or other, had some connection or other with salvation.

On Robertson of Brighton and William Law: Spurious spirituality is very dangerous.

Samuel Rutherford

Samuel Rutherford, in his work on *Christ Dying and Drawing Sinners to Himself* gives us some unpretending but deep philosophy. He denies power in the will against the Arminian, and asserts it against the Antinomian, position. And any other doctrine of power uncreaturifies the creature. It either brutifies man or deifies him.

Shorter Sayings

Thomas Shepard

Shepard is fine, but I wish I were as good as one of his hypocrites!

Richard Whately

I once heard Archbishop Whately, to my great disappointment. He was very dull and wishy washy. He preached on good behaviour, but it was blanched morality.

Herman Witsius

Herman Witsius . . . perhaps the most tender, spiritually-minded and richly evangelical, as well as one of the most learned of Dutch divines of the old (Dordrechtian) school.

Witsius and Halyburton

Witsius and Halyburton were, I should say, Owenians; yet they were not so great as Owen. They were minor men; yet we get nearer to them somehow.

Dr Duncan's Advice to Theologians

I would say to the theologian: Be biblical first of all; study the biblical, then study the ecclesiastical.

To theologize well you must cultivate a sense of the infinite evil of sin and of yourself as a sinner.

THEOLOGY

It is the fashion of our time to decry systematic theology, but that is tantamount to the dislike of science.

God created the world, and infant philosophy began; God created the Bible, and infant theology began.

We must systemise all our knowledge. We must keep our faith orderly.

Our systems of theology must be bondage till they are adopted on rational conviction.

A narrow theology, founded on the theologian's idiosyncrasies, is after all no theology at all.

Its Content Summarized

God, the law, sin, grace, Jesus the Mediator between God and sinners, and again the law.

Its Divisions

Polemical Theology is the defence, Practical Theology is the application, of Dogmatic Theology, which again rests upon Exegetical.

Theological Error and Heresy

All errors are abused truths. But then half a truth is also at the same time half a lie.

All error is not heresy.

A man may veer far from the centre, and yet his error never ripen into a heresy.

No man can be charged with heresy, even on a fundamental, till after faithful admonishment he persists in it, knowing that he does so.

Dr. Duncan and Theology

I am a philosophical sceptic who has taken refuge in theology.

My philosophy is under-propped by theology.

TRUST

We are to grow in dependent insufficiency, and in the knowledge of him who makes sufficient.

Cherish trust in the Lord and diffidence in yourself.

Your time is wholly in his hands, and his time is the best.

TRUTH

Platonism has to do with it – Christianity with *him*..

UNBELIEF

Conscience has no right to say to me, 'Though Christ died, you must die too. There can be no substitution, no transference of guilt, no transference of righteousness.' Conscience has no right to do that. It's an evil conscience that does that. Unbelief is reigning in the conscience, when conscience does that. There is a great deal of our unbelief *conscientious* unbelief. Conscience won't fully admit that God is pleased, that it may cast away its accusation and its demands, because of the obedience of Christ.

To a seeker: You say you cannot believe. I am glad you feel your inability. You cannot believe till you feel it.

Dr Duncan's confession: I am often at the nearest [or very near] point to fainting through not believing.

WILL

The older I grow, the subject of the human will seems more awful to me – the power to forsake God.

Man counts . . . God's will, as opposed to self-will, slavery; and self-will, as opposed to . . . the authority of God, that he counts liberty.

Paul's confession as to the contrary power within the will (*Rom.* 7:15, 18–21) is true also of the intellect, which the will leads as well as follows.

WOMEN

I have all my life been very dependent upon women, and much indebted to female society.

Female beauty is set forth in an architectural image: 'God built the woman' (*Gen.* 2:22).

Dr Duncan's housekeeper: Ah, well! Miss Sanderson was a blessing in this house. My house is emptier, but heaven is fuller.

WORLD

I don't much care for all the world becoming next-door neighbours.

We are drifting, drifting, drifting into an awfully materialistic and utilitarian age.

This is a world in which there is much to do, in which there is much of evil, much of ungodliness, and it needs many sharp tools.

Many of the Lord's people have very little of the world in possession, but they have it all in property, in Christ . . . Christ gives you the whole world in property, and as much in possession as he sees is good and best.

The world is a lost world. But the lost world is a divinity-visited world.

Considered Morally

There is anarchy. The world of mankind has cast off allegiance to its King.

What do you take the present state of the world to be? Why, we are under the ban of the empire.

Hateful haters! A world of hateful haters! Is not this world thus a forehall, an antechamber of hell?

Oh, the world likes a crowned Saviour tolerably well, if it were a crown without a cross, but a crucified Saviour – to draw men to be crucified!

The Church and the World

It is not the entire man frequently that the world hates – it is the new-born man . . . his union to Christ, his faith in Christ, his love to Christ, his devotion to Christ.

This is what to the world is the Christian's folly: losing the things that are seen for the things that are unseen, the things of time for the things of the eternal state.

Conformity to the world is one of the most besetting sins of the professing church at the present day.

Its Sin

'The sin of the world', of which the various sins are so many branches and manifestations, is the world's apostasy and alienation from the living God.

Every man is in the world's sin fundamentally . . . The whole world is in the sin. It involves me, it involves thee, it involves each individual.

Its Judgment

Here then is the judgment of the world. This world received not the Christ.

What will worldlings think when their god is all in a blaze?

[188]

Warnings and Exhortations

Beware of this world's philosophy and this world's rhetoric.

John 15:18: Christ's choice, the world's hate; put these two together, cleave to them in faith.

Transitory world, let it go! World that is not of the Father, let it go! Count it loss; count the loss of it gain.

Hate the world, yet hate not the world's men.

Love them that are in it, that they may be brought out of it.

Be not conformed to the world, in its sentiments, in its notions, in its views, in its pursuits.

WORSHIP

Whenever we worship, we acknowledge that there is a region above us, at once known and unknown, half-clear and half-dark.

We should fear, for Jesus is present, walking amidst the candlesticks to inspect.

The worship of the church on earth is conducted in heaven.

Jehovah is a God of wisdom, and he will have an intelligent worship.

We are to assemble to hear God's Word – but to what end? To do it.

I have no fear of the results of religious fervour in worship. Aberrations generally correct themselves in time. It is the total want of fervour that is lamentable.

PART II

Longer Extracts

ANTHEMS

I should like to have some anthems composed to suit certain passages from the Minor Prophets, which have been selected for that purpose. The musical notation to prose often brings out its poetry. We might have special anthems for all the prose poetry of Scripture. The Hebrew chanting is sometimes very grand. It is founded on the syntactical construction of the passages; the musical cadence giving rise to the accents, not the accents to the cadence or chant. Some Highland ministers chant their sermons; and the old Seceders used to sing them. Old Aitken of Kirriemuir sang like a very mavis. He had two tunes: his quotation tune, which he used as often as he could; and his ordinary one, for his own words. I have heard him sing, 'The Lord God of gods, the Lord God of gods, he knoweth, and Israel he shall know', as splendidly as they do it in the synagogue.

ASSURANCE

Three Elements of Assurance

With reference to the three opinions which you have mentioned in your leading article for last month as prevailing among evangelical Christians on the subject of assurance, I think there is truth in them all; but that each of them, if held exclusively of the others, is attended with its own danger. (For conciseness' sake let us call assurance by direct faith, No. 1; assurance by evidences of regeneration or marks of grace, No. 2; and assurance by the witness of the Spirit, No. 3.) Undoubtedly the danger of No. 1, held exclusively, is antinomianism; that of No. 2, held exclusively, is legalism; while if a man pretends to have the third without the first and second, it is either hypocrisy or the deepest self-delusion. Set up exclusively, they are each right against the others. But they can well agree. Yet I do not think they are three independent ways of assurance, nor so much three steps of a ladder to assurance, as three elements found by analysis to be contained in all true assurance. In fact, they constitute a living organism – No. 1 being analogous to the root, and No. 3 to the matured fruits of a tree; though indeed, as they come out in recognised experience, they are often like three steps of a ladder; and there must be always great delicacy in dealing with these theological relations in respect of living men, inasmuch as there may be morbid states of soul even in true Christians, and inasmuch also as some of the above-mentioned elements may in some souls be merely *seminal*.

Let us take them in order.

1. *Direct Faith – The First Element of Assurance*

Assurance by direct faith has, when held *ultra*, an element of truth, and also one of falsehood. Its element of truth is the plenitude and freedom of the gospel – Christ and his unsearchable riches offered to mankind-sinners as such.

Its element of falsehood appears when the necessity of regeneration unto faith is not exhibited, and we are represented as receiving Christ with the fallen hand of Adam; or where it is so held as to obstruct the way to No. 2 by putting aside such texts as these: 'If ye live after the flesh, ye shall die; but if ye through the Spirit do mortify the deeds of the body, ye shall live' (*Rom.* 8:13); 'They that are Christ's have crucified the flesh with the affections and lusts' (*Gal.* 5:24); or such as this, 'We must all appear before the judgment seat of Christ, that everyone may receive the things done in his body, according to that he hath done, whether it be good or bad' (2 *Cor.* 5:10). It is a bad faith that has not room for these texts. Faith has room for them; and if it is really faith, they will set us to self-examination.

I am afraid that assurance by direct faith is sometimes urged in a way to make men merely *infer* from their (real or supposed) faith that they have got what faith itself would actually get. Take the case of the woman who touched the hem of Christ's garment. There the faith was complete. She did not infer that because she believed she was healed. She *touched*. Then came a double experience: virtue went out of him; and she *felt* she was healed. When men merely infer they have got what a touch would really get, a false assurance is produced for the time, though conscience prevents its continuance; for nothing but the blood of Christ will satisfy the conscience. All this makes the question so tremendous.

2. *Marks of Grace; or, Reflection – The Second Element of Assurance*

I am not quite sure that the Bible speaks of what we call assurance by that name. It speaks of the full assurance of understanding (*Col.* 2:2), the full assurance of faith (*Heb.* 10:2), and the full assurance of hope (*Heb.* 6:2). But whether as meaning the same thing, or only connected with these, John in his first epistle calls it *knowing* – 'knowing that we know him' (*1 John* 2:3), and 'knowing that we have eternal life' (*1 John* 5:13). And what John says about this *knowing* appears to me to be most important, not only as specially written for the very purpose of producing this knowledge, but also as teaching us how we are to employ other Scriptures to the same purpose. John's first epistle is written co-relatedly to his gospel. The end of the gospel we have in the words, 'But these are written that ye might believe in the name of the Son of God, and that believing, ye might have life through his name' (*John* 20:31). The gospel, therefore, was written for the production of faith and the conveyance of life; whereas the object of the Epistle is given in the words, 'These things have I written *unto you that believe* on the name of the Son of God, that ye may *know that ye have* eternal life, *and that ye may believe* on the name of the Son of God' (*1 John* 5:13). This text implies three things: 1. That they who believe on the name of the Son of God *have* eternal life; 2. That they may be brought to the *knowledge* that they have eternal life; and 3. That this knowledge is not to supersede their living by direct faith on the Son of God; – in saying, 'And that ye may believe', etc.; it is as if he had said 'Now ye see what good ye have got by believing; therefore keep believing; yea, grow in grace, and in the knowledge of the Son of God; for ye see what good comes by believing.' This co-relation then between the gospel and the epistle seems very much to intimate that a man may believe on the Son of God and have life by his name, and yet need somewhat to help him to *know* that he has eternal life. The whole epistle presupposes the gospel; it presupposes faith in the Son of God, and the possession of life thereby, and then seeks to bring believers to the knowledge of their having eternal life by what are commonly called *marks of grace*[1] (our No.2).

Believing and receiving life is direct (No. 1); the knowledge that we believe and have life must have in it *reflection* upon ourselves (No. 2). And this reflection will embrace not only the actings of our faith, but its fruits; for the Spirit who works faith works all the concomitant graces (in such a way as always glorifies Christ); and these are cogniscible things.[2]

---

[1]David Brown's footnotes: 'I am not sure', remarked our venerable friend further on this point, 'but the whole may be resolved into the same principle with which the epistle begins. A message having been delivered as heard from Christ, that "God is light, and in him is no darkness at all" (*1 John* 1:5), it is applied, first, negatively, "If we say we have fellowship with him, and walk in darkness, we lie, and do not the truth" (verse 6), and then positively, "If we walk in the light as he is in the light, we have fellowship one with another, and the blood of Jesus Christ his Son cleanseth (is cleansing) us from all sin" (verse 7). This last clause is true, no doubt, as commonly used to show the all-sufficiency of the blood of Christ; but as used here, it is to show the actual cleansing.' *Pulpit and Communion Table*, Brown, p. 55.

[2]'Not cogniscible indeed by children', remarked our aged friend here, 'but adults have more reflection. A child cannot make his own mind the object of reflection; he thinks with his mind, but not about his mind. He is busy gazing on everything, a great subjectivity is going on, he is busy photographing; but he does not look at the (photograph). Therefore he may have faith, but he cannot come to the Lord's table, because he cannot examine himself as an adult can.'

'Do you not think', we asked him, 'that it is a misapplication of words when men contrast subjective with objective religion?' 'Yes; subjective religion is just intensely objective religion'. 'And what people really mean or censure or commend (as their views may be), by what they call subjectivity in religion, would be more properly called self-objectivity?' 'Perhaps.' *Pulpit and Communion Table*, Brown, p. 56.

Now Scripture attaches promises of life to the possession of these things, so that when I perceive them in myself I can reason in this way: God says, 'Believe in the Lord Jesus Christ, and thou shalt be saved'; but I believe in the Lord Jesus Christ; therefore I shall be saved. The major proposition of this syllogism is *God's* Word. But to have assurance of my salvation, I must be sure of my minor proposition also. I would like, therefore, to have two witnesses to it. If it is the testimony of my own conscience simply, it may be true; but the heart is deceitful. Now, 'the Spirit itself beareth witness with our spirit, that we are the children of God' (*Rom.* 8:16). This is our No. 3.

3. *The Witness of the Spirit – The Third Element of Assurance*

It seems to some to be enthusiastic and horrible; yet, considered doctrinally, it is the apex of this question; and *experimentally* it goes into the very essence of religion.

What is meant in the above-quoted verse by 'our spirit'? Is it merely our intelligent minds? It is that, but it is the spirit born of the Spirit. 'The Holy Spirit', says one of the Fathers, 'makes us *holy* and *spiritual*'. The testimony of God's Spirit, then, is only with the spirit of a regenerate man; it is the witness of the *regenerating* with the *regenerated* spirit.

['Oh, my leanness! my leanness!', interjected Dr Duncan at this point, 'No. 3 will lead us into the very core of Christianity, far, far beyond my experience. I have certainly more light about it than experience of it. Indeed, my light about it is flickering; but it goes beyond my experience – at least as interpreted and judged of by myself. Ah, yes!']

Not only does the Spirit of God bring out his own graces into vivid exercise (No. 1); and not only is he pleased, especially at times, to shine upon these – without which the believer's perception of them (No. 2) is dark and indistinct – this testimony is something more. It is the Father and the Son communicating with the souls of believers by the Holy Ghost, by means of the truth; and in this lies very mainly the secret of experimental religion. For example, prayer. The Spirit working sincerity, earnestness of desire, etc. – all that is contained in the 'inwrought prayer' of a Christian man – this Christian man may not only be conscious by his own spirit (namely, his regenerate soul) that he doth so pray; but, if the Father heareth and answereth prayer – that is, if there be as much reality in God's speaking to man as there is in man's speaking to God – then, as certainly as the believer has access by the Spirit through Christ unto the Father in presenting his supplication, so certainly the Father hath access through the Son by the Spirit that dwells in this man to convey the answer. Is this strange? Given a spiritual world – given a living God and (by regeneration) a living soul, is it incredible that there should be such intercourse between them; that the soul should speak to a hearing God, and hear a speaking God? This indeed is the very kernel of experiential religion; sending us to our closets; to our Father who seeth in secret, to be alone with God – where there is no voice audible by the outward ear, but yet a voice audible by the inner ear. For faith has an ear, as certainly as God has a mouth; though if we be asked, 'How do you know that God speaks to you?', we could only answer, 'Because I hear him'. It is like asking a man, 'Why do you believe your senses?'

Now, then, to full assurance, we need a particular *saying* of God to our individual souls ('*Say* unto my soul', was David's prayer, 'I am thy salvation'); and this, to a man without faith, and without fruits of faith, he will never say. But wherever faith (No. 1) is – implying, as it does, regeneration, or good seed in good ground – it will be certainly followed by discernible fruits (No. 2), and by the witness of the Spirit (No. 3). Faith is *seminal* of all.

Whom to Suspect

I have said that there is great delicacy in applying these relations to the cases of living men who may be in a morbid state, or in whom some of the elements may as yet be merely seminal. I am not suspicious, therefore, of professing Christians merely because they want assurance of their own salvation; neither, on the other hand, am I suspicious of the assurance of young converts; for I believe God may give assurance as soon as he gives faith. But I am suspicious of the profession of assurance and high joy when it is without any indication of brokenness and contriteness of heart; when it is without the solemnizing of character which a view of God's tremendous wrath and great salvation must give; and when it is without docility – when young converts set up to be teachers – and various other things. I can conceive a man or woman, boy or girl, coming home from church and telling us they had found Christ, and I would not doubt it; or telling me so, and I would doubt it much.

I think I saw during the late revival[1] two great evils –

[1]The reference is to what David Brown calls, 'The remarkable "Revival" movement' which swept over a large part of Scotland – beginning about the close of the year 1858, rising to some height in the next two years, and continuing, though with less "observation", for several years thereafter.'

first, an over-suspicion in old professors (who may have been old believers) regarding the young converts; and *secondly,* a foolish, rash, presumptuous judgment on the part of the young converts; going almost to make out that those who had long consistently professed the gospel of Christ were no believers at all, because they had not that apparent, ardent, and high assurance that these young people had. Yet even these corrupt elements led me only to a suspicion, not to a negation of those young professors; for I believe that there may be some true faith incrusted with a vast deal of presumption, and that the whole being taken for faith bulks very much in their esteem, and that when it is peeled off their faith won't appear so very big. I believe there may be some God-made faith and man-made faith in the same soul. However, 'Every branch in me', saith Christ, 'that beareth fruit, he purgeth it, that it may bring forth more fruit.' After the scythe will come the dew – the 'rain on the mown grass'.

Of the doctrine that will allow none to be true believers who want full assurance of their own salvation, Andrew Gray of Glasgow (if I remember right) says, 'It is more discouraging than the dark and doubtsome faith of the Papists.' I have much sympathy with doubts which arise from a high estimate of Christian character as set forth in the scriptural delineations of what all true believers (regenerate men) are, and, in contrast therewith, from a low view of their own attainments, that stimulates while it humbles. There are, however, it is to be feared, those who by a latent Popery, 'the pride which apes humility', make their doubts a part, and no small part, of their religion. Others again there are with consciences partially enlightened, with a glimmer which hinders them from being at ease in grossest self-delusion, but not sufficiently penetrating and arousing to stir them to honest effort, who sink into a state of dull apathy or fretful despondency. Such should be warned to look well to it, that their self-suspicions be not too well grounded. The only way to be taken with such doubts is, honestly, manfully, resolutely, in the sight of God, and by the light of his Word to face them, that by his grace they may, if found groundless, be dismissed; or if found well-grounded, the removal of the doubts be sought by the removal of their causes, in the way of betaking themselves to the all-sufficient, freely-offered Saviour of sinners. Other way of relief know I none (*Prov.* 13:4; 15:19; 21:25). Whether assurance be or not be, in the present state of the professing church, a *rare attainment*, I know not; but I am convinced that no good, but on the contrary only much harm, can accrue from further letting down of the duly moderated doctrine of all the Protestant churches, that *fidelis potest et debet esse certus de sua salute* – ' a believer can and should be sure of his own salvation' – that is, in the way of giving all diligence, which it may be feared is *too rare an effort*.

BELIEVERS

Whose are We?

Whose are we? Are we our own? Do we hold ourselves our own? Do we feel as if we were still our own? Do we act as if we were our own? Whose will is the rule of our conduct, our own or Christ's? Whose cause do we make ours, our own or Christ's? On whose interests are we oftenest and most ardently looking, our own or Christ's?

Where would we be most willingly? Would we be where Christ is – here in his ordinances, or above in his personal presence? Or would we be where Christ is not? What troubles us most? Is it dishonour to Christ? What pleases us most? Is it glory given to Christ? What glory do we give to him? How do we give it? Is it with our spirits and with our bodies? If we are not Christ's, whose are we? Our own. And if we be our own, we have a poor proprietor – a poor proprietor. What are we to make of ourselves? How are we to dispose of ourselves? How are we to get through life? 'Oh,' you say, 'that can be managed.' Well, but at death, and at the judgment-seat, and throughout eternity, how are we to manage for ourselves, if we be our own? Ah! But if we should present the claim to be our own, there is one that will scoff and mock. 'Thine own! Poor deluded one! Thou art mine.' You have heard of 'the god of this world', of 'the spirit that now worketh in the children of disobedience'. 'Mine, mine,' he says; 'Jesus I know, he hath made an invasion of my dominions, and carried captivity captive, but – save him – I can laugh at the poor deluded, enslaved race. Mine, mine. They are the world's, and the world is mine.' And now, who hath the best master? Which is the best master? The world and the world's god, or the Christ of God, Christ who is God? Who hath the best master, the wordling thou – or the saints?

CHRIST

His Errand into the World

I ask, what was Christ's errand into the world? For surely our errand into the world must be deeply connected with his. And I often think of that saying of his, 'It is more blessed to give than to receive', in connection not only with our duty to others, but with our duty to him. We must not only imitate him, we must concede to him this superior blessedness of giving to us. And the noblest thing a man can do is just humbly to receive, and then to go amongst others and give. I've not been able to give much. It's because I have received so little. And if there is anything in which I would be inclined to contradict him it would be if I heard him say, 'Well done, good and faithful servant'.

His Death

'And as it is appointed unto men once to die, but after this the judgment: so Christ was once offered to bear the sins of many; and unto them that look for him shall he appear the second time without sin, unto salvation.' Amidst all the deaths that have taken place, there is one that stands out distinct and pre-eminent above them all. We die, because we are sinners; we die, because we sinned in the first of men; we die, having added innumerable actual transgressions, sin having abounded. But there died One who was holy, harmless, undefiled, and separate from sinners; One who did no violence, neither was deceit found in his mouth; One of whom the Heavenly Father proclaimed, 'This is my beloved Son, in whom I am well pleased'; and One who was not involved in the guilt of Adam's transgression, for he came not by ordinary generation.

His Arrows

'His arrows are sharp in the heart of his enemies.' Alas! that I should be an enemy to my best friend, and fight against my own salvation. He hath sent some arrows of his terrors, and I was (in a measure) distracted. This morning he sent an arrow of love, and it was sharper still, for it is the text, 'The blood of Christ shall purge your conscience'. May the arrow dipt in the life's blood of the Son of God be fixed to remain for ever, and my whole soul brought in subjection to him – his blood, at once my soul's redemption and purgation, carried into the holiest of all, as atoning – sprinkled on my conscience, cleansing. 'There is one Lawgiver, who is able to save and to destroy.' Pray for me, dear friend, who am sometimes trembling exceedingly before him as able to destroy, sometimes a little helped, as I judge, to trust in him as able to save, and wishful to be brought by his grace to the harmonious exercise of both together.

His Drawing Power

Christ crucified, that's the Object drawing – drawn to it – drawn away from all that is not Christ, drawn to Christ – drawn to him in his Person, covenant-engagements, work, gospel, law, grace, authority – drawn to him as your Prophet, and Priest, and King – as all your salvation and all your desire. Are you being drawn? Drawn more and more? If Christ has been drawing you, sure I am he has not finished drawing you. We are not so near Jesus as we should be, as we must be, as, if we are under his drawing, we shall be. All who have been drawn are being drawn still; and all who have been drawn and are being drawn are approximating, are coming to Christ. They have heard him who says 'Come!' and they have set out to go to him, and they're going, going; and he is always saying 'Come, come!' and they're coming and getting nearer.

What steps of progress are we making as the results of this drawing? Surely, surely if we are not coming, he is not drawing. He is drawing in one sense, in his sweet and powerful invitations, but so drawing as that we feel able to resist them all still. Surely there is another drawing than that, a drawing not to be resisted. Are we drawn by that drawing? There is a drawing with the cords of love and the bands of a man. Sweet affections, different from all constraints and contraries, but stronger than all constraints – more powerful than all necessity – the constraint of love. What stumbling-blocks in the way are you getting over? What other attractions are being loosed and letting you on? What bands untied? What swiftness given to the feet, making them like hinds' feet? What kindling up of the love strong as death, and the jealousy cruel as the grave? What sacrifices, what accounting of all things but loss for the excellency of Jesus Christ? What suffering for his sake of the loss of all things, and counting them but dung if so be we may win Christ and be found in him? Feel you ever his attractive power coming and drawing hard away from detentions? When you are slow, and he goes away, putting in his hand at the hole of the door, and leaving the smell of the sweet myrrh, what meetings of heart – what openings even for the gone Beloved – and, when he is not found, what rising and going about the city? What drawing to a crucified Saviour? Oh, the world likes a crowned Saviour tolerably well, if it were a crown without a cross, but a crucified Saviour – to draw men to be crucified! A crown without a cross for me, saith the natural heart. Jesus is drawing you to the cross.

Longer Extracts

A Call to Look to Christ

Oh, for such a look of Christ as will scatter sin. Oh, for such a discovery of his glory as will draw forth love to him! Oh, for such a sight of him as will never let the eye off from him again – such a sight as would make us follow him through good report and through bad report, through life and through death – such a sight of him as would lead us to seek to be with him where he is, that we may behold his glory! Oh, for such a sight of the Lamb of God as would make it the soul's perpetual exercise ever to look! Oh, to have our sins washed away in his precious blood, our crimson stains that we might be whiter than the snow! He took away sin – he died once for the expiation, but oh! the accomplishment is going on through the ages of time, rolling on, the accomplishment of what he did, the application of it, the communication of pardon and purity and peace. Once for all he took away our sins by expiation, but he is for ever taking away sins by the application. Oh, for applications! Believers, I trust you have brought your sins with you to the Lord, to the fountain opened for sin and for uncleanness. I hope you have brought your sins with you to give them to Christ, to take them away from you. Look now, behold him now, through all your pilgrimage on earth; behold him till you come at last through the Jordan of death. 'Behold the Lamb of God!' That light shines from heaven, that light guides you. Oh, walk in him!

Coming to Christ

For myself, I cannot always come to Christ direct, but I can always come by sin. Sin is the handle by which I get

Christ. I take a verse in which God has put Christ and sin together. I cannot always put my finger upon Christ and say, 'Christ belongs to me'; but I can put my finger upon sin and say, 'Sin belongs to me.' I take the word, for instance, 'The Son of man is come to save that which was lost.' Yes, lost, lost – I'm lost; I put my finger upon that word and say, 'I'm the lost one; I'm lost.' Well, I find that 'the Son of man is come to save the lost'; and I cry out, 'What God hath joined together, let not man put asunder.'

Contemplating Christ

'Behold the Lamb of God'

But these words direct us to the *contemplation* of the Lamb of God. Not to a simple glance; although we should be glad if we could get sinners so to honour Christ. For we are sure that the eye that sees him once would never cease to gaze on him. We know that people have their thoughts in a certain way about Christ, which they can take up and lay down, which they get ready for any specific purposes of their own; but these are not views of Christ at all. If they saw him, he is not an object to let the eye off. Do you think that the King in his beauty, if once but a glimpse were obtained of him – that his beauties would not fix the gaze? When, O soul! will you have seen all the beauty of Christ? When will you have fathomed the depth of purity and love and grace that's but in one only of his words of eternal life? When will you have scrutinized his gracious heart, so as to say, 'I have searched to the bottom, and I know it all'? When will you have given but a cursory glance to his unsearchable riches, and say, 'Now, I have at least taken the inventory and catalogue of them all'? Friends, God hath provided an eternal heaven for us in his own Lamb. He is Heaven's heaven. There could not be an eternity of blessedness without an object of highest, holiest contemplation. We should weary in course of revolving ages of anything which hath a limit of any excellence, of which we could say, 'Now this is exceeding good: for the last million of years I have enjoyed it all!' What kind of Christians then are they who are pleased with a glance of Christ? What can we say of the eye which turns from him, but that it has never seen him, else diversion of the eye were an impossibility? What can we say of ourselves if he gets a passing thought among other objects at our leisure and convenience? Oh, surely we have not seen him. Behold, then, the Lamb of God! Behold him! The Father's eye never ceases resting on him with delight! And what are the demands of the Father for excellence, that his eye can rest upon him with eternally unwearied delight! The blessed Spirit hath never wearied through thousands of years of the one unchanging work of glorifying him, and what must be the excellence of that subject which occupies the Holy Spirit of God with never wearied delight to reiterate! The whole church of God hath been looking from the beginning, and tire it never shall, neither of the exercise nor in it. The eyes of the glorified shall through eternity rest on this Object. Therefore let us contemplate Christ.

Looking to Christ

This vision, this contemplation of the Lamb of God, is unspeakably full of blessedness to the persons contemplating. Keep this motive in its right place. Ah! If we truly see the Lamb of God, the blessedness of our souls in the vision will be but a secondary consideration. His glory, his beauty, his grace will fill the soul. It will produce devotion, and what's devotion? Is it the seeking to gather in and to gain and get? No! It's the going out, the desire to give, whilst the sinner's consciousness that he hath nothing worthy only humbles him. I am not speaking of him taking him to save him, but of taking him as an acknowledgment of his goodness in permitting him to look, to adore, to offer up his body and soul a living sacrifice, acceptable to God through Christ Jesus. If we truly behold Christ, his goodness will produce this frame of mind. But still it is true, and has its own place, that the contemplation of Christ is full of blessedness to the soul. Yes, beholding the Lamb of God, we see the Father shining in his face. We see God. We have the blessedness of the pure in heart. 'He that hath seen Me hath seen the Father.' We behold the holy God, the righteous God, the God that taketh vengeance, pacified, smiling, acquiescing, delighted. We behold God in Christ reconciling the world to himself, not imputing unto men their trespasses. We learn, with deepest consciousness of sin, with profoundest reverence of divine purity, to approach God as conscious sinners of the deepest dye with holy confidence. We can draw near with loads of guilt, like universes piled up upon us, with consciousness of pollution unutterable, and hell-stains upon our hearts, and look up to God, and see mercy and grace and love, whilst holiness and justice are maintained. We thus obtain peace – peace in contemplating the Lamb of God – peace of conscience which flows from beholding God just when justifying the ungodly, and are enabled to cast our ungodliness, with freeness of heart, or, if not freeness of heart, with unsuspecting confidence.

COMMUNION OF SAINTS

I am glad that Dr Bonar has been going into what, I think, we are greatly behind in – the communion of saints. Who are comprehended in the communion of saints? Some of them are more than believers now. Is it not the whole family that in heaven and earth is named of the Father' (*Eph.* 3:14, 15)? Did you ever thank God for Abel's five thousand years of heaven? It is an exercise of faith to know that Abel has been five thousand years in heaven; but 'if one member rejoice, all the members rejoice with it'. We ought to rejoice for Abel and Abraham and Job and David. We forget the best part of the church when we forget the church triumphant. You say we cannot see it; and that is the difficulty, because it is an act of pure faith and love. The saints on earth – we can to them express our faith and love; we can do them good as we have opportunity; to the saints in heaven we can do none of these things. Also, of the blessedness which they enjoy we very imperfectly know. But am I not to rejoice that they are most blessed – with a blessedness beyond my highest powers to comprehend? In being beyond the power of my comprehension, is it rendered beyond the power of my faith and love? Nay, more, does not faith invoke the Saviour as 'him that is able to do abundantly above all that we ask or think'? – to do for us, and so much more for them. But the communion of saints is in this world defective – it is a grace which with regard to the saints in heaven can be exercised only in faith and love: they can do us no good and we can do none to them. Still there is no doubt that they take an interest in us. When Paul had departed to be with Christ, which was far better, I suppose he had not ceased to care for the church on earth – the militant church. There is little said about it, but let us look at it soberly, as we may be able. Does no news go between earth and heaven? And if news goes, must there not be a knowledge of events? God has put there a veil: Popery tries to bring us within it, and Protestants will not look at it for Papistical abuse. Between us and the Father and the Son there is a fellowship in faith and supreme love; also there is a fellowship between us and the saints in subordinate love. The one is an exercise in filial love toward God, and the other an exercise of subordinate love toward the saints – the glorified as well as the militant: take in the best part of the church in your idea of the church. It may be you have that which may be the foundation for faith and love where there can be communion in no other way. If I can love a saint in America, whom I have never seen – nay, if I can in the exercise of pure faith love all the people of God, whom I have never known – say that the saints are not in America but in heaven, will that put them out, though it be in a purely spiritual exercise? Is a man not my neighbour because he has gone to the upper flat? It is very difficult to exercise a fellowship that has nothing of sense. The saints in heaven – we have not seen them; but God has told us about them, we believe that they are the same family, and we hope to meet together. Dr Kidd, who with all his roughness had a great deal of spiritual-mindedness about him, used to say, 'Well, when you go to heaven, which you hope to do, what will you have to say to David? What will you have to say to Paul?' And so on.

CONSCIENCE

Conscience and the Right of Access to God

Conscience, in imputing to me my sin, acts for God. It hath no right to let go its claim until it hear from God, the Supreme Judge. When he receives satisfaction, conscience is bound to acquiesce in his declaration, and to give up its claim and its condemnation and its pursuit, and thus to set me free from this great barrier which interposed between me and access to God in his worship – namely, conscience of sins. It is, 'therefore', because of this perfect offering – 'having *therefore*, brethren, boldness to enter into the holiest by the blood of Jesus'.

The term 'boldness to enter into the holiest' in this verse, we do not understand *subjectively* – that is to say, with regard to the temper and feeling of our souls; but *objectively*, having a free and unfettered right of access against which there is no barrier – having a door opened, nothing repelling – having invitation and free access and ground of hope: for to understand the words otherwise would be to confound the privilege with the duty which follows upon it, and which is set forth in the words, 'Let us draw near', etc.

CONVERSION

Instantaneous Conversion

I believe that a man may come into a new world consciously, in an instant of time, and that through no specific agency. But I must equally affirm that in the very nature of things the three elements stated in our

Catechism as parts of 'effectual calling' are essentially necessary – the 'conviction of sin', the 'enlightening in the knowledge of Christ', and the 'renewing of the will'. They are terms of a sequence. Thus, 'conviction' may be pungent, may be *ever so pungent*, yet come short of the off-cutting, the cutting off of the legal hope: that belongs to the 'enlightenment in the knowledge of Christ'. And this, again, may be keen, may be terribly vivid, and yet 'the will' remain unpliant and unrenewed. I believe that the act of 'renewal' is instantaneous; but there is a power as well as an act, and in its development to the observation of others, or even to a man's own consciousness, it may be slowly progressive. In the Philippian jailer, in Nicodemus, in Cornelius, in Nathanael, you see the instantaneousness of the act, and Nathanael was a man truly renewed before he had heard the facts of the life of Christ, and Cornelius was a renewed man before Peter saw him.

DEATH

Address after the Death of William Cunningham (1861)

Dear Young Gentleman, – Gathered together this day in the name of our Lord Jesus, who has promised his presence, we meet in peculiar circumstances – solemn, afflictive, trying, that is, probatory. The Lord hath taken our master from our head. His immense gain is our great loss. We love him too well to indulge the wish that it were otherwise. We thank the Lord who gave us so great a boon and now he hath taken him to be with himself, which is far better, greater is the ground for our sympathetic joy than for our lawful, reasonable, and dutiful grief on our own account.

The Head of the great school in which all Zion's children are taught of God, said, when about to depart, 'If ye loved me ye would rejoice, because I go to my Father'; and the analogy of the Head is applicable to the members.

I will not venture, nor do I need, to speak of what is so well known throughout all Scotland, and far beyond it. I will not say in praise of him, but of him who endowed him with natural abilities so vigorous and so fine, and with grace so early, so abundantly; forming him to be in so distinguished a degree a good and faithful servant, a diligent and affectionate pastor, a good soldier of Jesus Christ, who with wise and tender love for the persons of all men, used mercilessly the might which Christ had given him only against error and sin, pernicious to man as dishonouring to God.

Of him as a Professor I need say nothing to you who have studied under him. We, his bereaved colleagues, deeply feel our loss. Chalmers is gone from me. Cunningham is gone from me – with mine eyes to the Forerunner, I would say *before* me. They have gone, but they have left names and remembrances sweet, fragrant, hallowed; to me, indeed, deeply humbling yet animating – a sweet savour of Christ, of him who saith, 'Come unto me, all ye that labour and are heavy laden, and I will give you rest'; who also says, 'Be thou faithful unto the death, and I will give thee a crown of life.'

Cunningham being dead yet speaketh. One not girding on his armour but about to put it off, and exchange the battle-field for the victory which the Captain of salvation having achieved, bestows, leaves us (with his example commended by *itself*, not himself) a word, very precious and endeared the more to us by the death-bed and dying lips from which it comes – a word so consoling, so animating:

> *A few short years of evil past*
> *We reach the happy shore*
> *Where death-divided friends at last*
> *Shall meet, to part no more.*

DEBT

The Great Debtor

O my soul, how much thou owest! Ten thousand talents. 'When they had nothing to pay, he frankly forgave them.' 'Much hath been forgiven her – she loved much.' O my soul! What is thy desire? The great forgiveness and the great love.

O my soul, let the forgiveness enter thy conscience, it will introduce the love into thy heart.

O my soul, thy forgiveness must be great forgiveness, not only absolutely but comparatively.

O my soul, let the great forgiveness permeate they conscience, and it will inflame thy heart.

O my soul, grieve not the Holy Spirit inviting thee to this: he will enable thee – even now.

Prayerfully, watchfully, confidingly, wait and aim: he will enable thee more and more.

In him who desires union to the Lord Jesus above all things – but, O my soul! Dost thou so? If I cannot say so without much jealousy, which may not all be self-jealousy,

I dare not in the sight of God say, No; much rather, Yes. Lord, do Thou determine the question! – In him who desires union to the Lord first above all things, doubt of the forgiveness is agonising to himself and dishonouring to Christ.

If thy conscience will not have the forgiveness (that is, as a thing to enter into it as its content), then Christ cannot have the great love.

Great debt contracted [is the] great debtor's danger – great debtor's fear. Great debtor's rich Friend, [the] rich Friend's payment [of the debt], and [the] great debtor's free pardon procured. Pardon bought with blood put into the great debtor's hand (conscience – conscience – conscience!). Great debtor's new debt. Great debtor's heart peaceful, grateful, loving, devoted. What shall I render!

EFFECTUAL CALLING

Effectual Calling and the Free Offer of the Gospel

Question 31: Effectual calling is the work of God's Spirit, whereby, convincing us of our sin and misery, enlightening our minds in the knowledge of Christ, and renewing our wills he doth persuade and enable us to embrace Jesus Christ, freely offered to us in the gospel (Shorter Catechism).

(1) It is *Christ* that is offered; (2) He is *freely* offered; (3) It is in the gospel that he is freely offered. The word 'gospel' is used sometimes in a wider, sometimes in a more restricted sense. The 'gospel' may mean and embrace the whole of the New Testament revelation: it may also be put

widely for the whole revelation of God, so far as given with evangelical design and tendency. In its wider sense, the gospel comprehends narrative, testimony, promise, doctrine; but also commands and threatenings – all that appertains to or is connected with the gospel. But strictly so called, the gospel is God's testimony concerning his Son – his Gift of Jesus Christ as the appointed Saviour. Hence the gospel, in the strictest sense, hath no commands or threatenings. There is a command of God that we believe in the name of Christ; but this properly belongs to the head of law – a law of God in regard to the gospel. And that law hath a threatening – 'He that believeth not shall be damned'. This, then, is the gospel strictly: 'The Son of Man is come to seek and to save that which was lost'; 'Christ died, the just for the unjust, that he might bring us to God'; 'This is a faithful saying, and worthy of all acceptation, that Christ Jesus came into the world to save sinners, of whom I am chief'; 'Whom God hath set forth to be a propitiation through faith in his blood'; 'I have given him to be a Witness to the people'. Such passages contain simply and purely gospel – good news.

Other passages, where faith is mentioned, are two-fold: one class exhibiting our warrant to believe in Christ: and this faith which bringeth salvation may be held as belonging to the head of 'gospel' strictly so called. But passages which put faith in the light of obligation belong rather to the head of the law which God hath made about the gospel. Thus I take the precision of language on the part of the 'Marrow-men', who were in the main on the side of gospel truth – if it be not carried to captiousness; for that too is a fault – construing loose language as if it were grave error: these make such passages as this –

'Believe on the Lord Jesus Christ, and thou shalt be saved', in so far as Christ *saves,* to be pure gospel; but in so far as believing is by the authority of God, which binds men to believe, they hold it to belong to the head of law. So, in texts where 'faith' occurs, they distinguish between the *gospel* and the *law of the gospel.* The gospel contains the *doctrine* of salvation and the sinner's *warrant* to believe. It is in the gospel that Christ is offered, and that is the warrant for our faith.

We must beware of substituting any other warrant for trusting in Christ than the gospel. Christ must have the place given to him, the Spirit the place given to him, the gospel the place given to it. The work of the Spirit – in convincing, enlightening, enabling to believe in Christ – must never be put as our warrant to believe in Christ. The formal reason must not be because we are convinced, enlightened, persuaded; that is not the ground why we trust, but simply that he is revealed to us in the gospel. Christ is the object of saving faith, and God in him; the Spirit is the efficient Cause, the word of the truth of the gospel is the Warrant. In believing on Christ we do it not on the ground of any speciality, but on the ground of that which is common to us with mankind. Thus all self-confidence is guarded against. A sinner convinced is no more *entitled* to believe by his being convinced than an unconvinced sinner – the enlightened, the persuaded, no more than if they were not so. Nothing that distinguishes from all the world, or from any other men, can give us a title; and for this very good reason that a full title is given independent of all that. If it were otherwise, the doctrine of *merit* is introduced the moment that is admitted. In short, we obscure and destroy the glorious gospel of the grace of God, and its absolute freeness, unless we take in that not only is it no presumption to believe, but that it is a positive law. All such ideas of warrant resting upon a certain condition of mind is pernicious, as a dark cave for a soul to retreat into and defend itself against the authority of God to command faith.

I once had a discussion on this point with a person in the West Highlands, a man of considerable knowledge, and not without seriousness. I asked, was Christ offered to *him*? He was silent. To whom, then, was he offered? He answered to those wishing to receive him. Now that was a complete subterfuge. So long as a man is in that condition of mind he is inexpugnable. If Christ were offered only to the *wishing*, then in not being willing there can be no unbelief, for there is no offer. If there be in the gospel a real offer of Christ, then is there in the gospel that which demands, on the hearing of it, the acting of human volition. Every hearing of the gospel demands human volition. A reception by one involves the alternative of rejection by those who receive it not. Which do we do? To deal honestly in offering it to others, we must first have received it ourselves.

Although it be true that the elect only believe unto salvation, yet it is the convinced sinner, as such, and not the elect sinner, as such, that savingly believes. Yet the gospel being offered to all mankind sinners, God's elect, in believing, do condemn the world of unbelievers, because they receive Christ on no special ground, but offered to them as, and in common with, others. The work of God's Spirit, in convincing of sin and misery, enlightening the mind in the knowledge of Christ, renewing the will, and persuading and enabling them to embrace Christ, is special to God's elect: but their being saved is not on the *ground* of their being so, but because they believe on Jesus Christ as perishing sinners like others.

Let us put this to ourselves first, and to the people next. Shall we condemn the world of the unbelieving? Or shall the company of believers condemn us? If the truth be as we put it, either every believing man should condemn me, for he believed on what was common to us both, or else I should condemn every unbelieving man for I believed what would have saved them if they had believed it. Let us mark how the gospel presses upon human volition. I speak not now of difficulties which may be raised to the [extent of the] Atonement, but I would that we should remember that what is offered is not a *doctrine* but a *Person*. If it be the case that Christ invites every sinner to his fellowship and salvation, inviting all, and promising to save every coming sinner, then clearly there must of necessity be the act of the will. If there were but a bare doctrine, veracity only would have to be considered; but here there is the social act of trusting.

How glorious a plan is the blessed gospel! So free that it secures the salvation of every hearer of the gospel, provided he be not a rejector of it! The gospel saves all who hear it – save those who reject it. It saves none but by positive reception: none are lost but by positive rejection of it. Men evangèlized cannot go to hell but over the bowels of God's great mercies. They must wade to it through the blood of Christ, and trample that blood under foot. And what an act of contempt against the Persons of the Godhead! Oh, what strength is in the human will! How great power men have to put away the grace of the gospel!

But we cannot *help* dealing with the gospel. It necessitates that we deal with it every time it comes in contact with us: every hearing of it must be attended, on our part, either by faith or by unbelief. And if it contain an offer of Christ, then unbelief comprehends not only rejection by the understanding as to testimony, but the action of the will as regards the offer. And the belief in the gospel is not simply a belief that the offer is made, but an embracing of that offer – not merely a belief that Jesus is the Christ, and that if I take him I shall be saved, but an actual receiving of him, a willingness to *have*, corresponding with his believing willingness to *give*.

If these things be so, you see what lies suspended on the action of the human will. And yet, if all were left to fallen man, the multitudes and the word of God show how it would be. The fact that the willingness to receive the gospel, though it be a fair demand of God on his fair offer, is brought out to be the fruit of the renovation of a man's will by the Holy Ghost, shows how it would be. And so the two ends of the question begin to come together: the man is thus 'persuaded and enabled to embrace Jesus Christ, freely offered to him in the gospel'.

We have thus seen some outline of the gospel – what it is, its bearing on human volition, necessitating an alternative of faith or unbelief in all who hear it.

ESTABLISHMENT PRINCIPLE

I can quite distinguish between the Establishment principle and endowments. It is the duty of the civil magistrate –

be it a Despotism, I don't mean in a bad sense, be it an Oligarchy, be it a Republic, but a moral unit – to see that Christianity be taught to all his subjects. But it may not be his duty in all circumstances to endow the church. If the church can teach the people without endowment, he may let it do so; but it is his duty to see that it be done. This is a Protestant country: if Queen Victoria were not a Protestant, she would have no right to reign, and if the Prince of Wales were not, he would have no right to succeed. But I believe the Protestant succession will be assailed too. *Miss R.* – 'About the Catholic Emancipation Bill, when the Catholics pay taxes, would it be unjust to shut them out from representation?'; *Dr Duncan* – 'If it be a civil *right*, it would be unjust to deprive them of it; but if it be a *trust*, those only should be put into it who are trustworthy.'

EXTERMINATION OF THE CANAANITES

Is the command to exterminate the Canaanites consistent with perfect moral right and justice? Well, we are subjects, not the lords of our own actions and lives. The Canaanite life was a forfeited life, specially so, because of special sin. God then had certainly a right to uproot their tribes. [Comment by a hearer: 'That is clear enough. But the question is, had a *man* a right to do so?'] Man delegated by God, to do so. All turns upon that. A supreme ruler need not always act himself, but may delegate his wishes to a subordinate. But the jurisdiction emanates from headquarters. It is Victoria that hangs. No British life is taken away judicially, but she indirectly sentences to death. And the subordinates all *represent* her. The Statute-book even says that if a hangman can't be found, the Sheriff, representing royalty, must undertake the duties of the executioner.

FAITH

Scrutinizing One's Faith

Sandy Macleod of Bracadale was acceptable to 'the men', though in his preaching he directed them most to Christ and the Bible. Once at a 'question meeting' they had been discussing the distinction between true and counterfeit faith. When they were done he said, 'All that is very well, but in analysing and scrutinizing your faith there is danger of neglecting the Object of faith. Was your faith crucified for you? Or were ye baptized in the name of your faith?' It is of more consequence that I eat my dinner than that I inquire into the state of my digestion. God maintains life in me without my always thinking about or being conscious of my vital organs performing their functions. So the Holy Spirit maintains spiritual life in me without my always thinking about or being conscious of the actings of life in my soul. Doctors inquire into and scrutinize the vital organs and their actings, but they live themselves like other people. I remember in my youth reading a book on physiology which interested me; now it turned out that the author's theory was quite wrong, yet he lived himself just in the way that others did. There are plain, simple Christians who do live spiritually, yet they do not know or think much about the inward actings of spiritual life. And there are divines, ministers, or persons who are divines, who scrutinize and analyse faith and the actings of faith.'

GOD

His Adorable Excellence

You have learned in your Catechism, 'What is God?'
And the answer is: 'God is a Spirit, infinite, eternal and
unchangeable in his being, wisdom, power, holiness,
justice, goodness, and truth'. These perfections of God
are distinguished into his communicable and incommunicable perfections. His incommunicable perfections
are infinity, eternity, and immutability; and he is infinite,
eternal, and unchangeable in all his perfections – in his
communicable perfections. His communicable perfections are wisdom, power, holiness, justice, goodness,
and truth; and among these, the communicable perfections of God, we may distinguish between the two first –
wisdom and power – and the others, which are most
properly called God's moral perfections – holiness,
justice, goodness and truth. For wisdom, considered
simply as intellect, and if not conjoined with moral
perfection, is the wisdom that is 'earthly, sensual, devil-
ish'; and so with power, considered simply in itself. But
wisdom and power in God are holy, just, and good
wisdom and power, and are in God as infinite, eternal,
and unchangeable wisdom, power, holiness, justice,
goodness and truth. In creating rational spirits, angels,
and men, God communicated to them not only being –
finite and changeable being, wisdom, and power, but
also the other perfections, which we more strictly call the
moral perfections of God – holiness, justice, goodness,
and truth. And in these lies, fundamentally, the amiableness of God, which mounts up by the incommunicable

perfections of infinity, eternity, and unchangeableness, into not only amiableness but adorable excellence.

Knowing that He is God

'Be still and know that I am God'

What, then, are you called to do in this stillness? To know that Jehovah is God, to know that the created universe is not all that exists, that there is something else than all that ever was made, than all that rolls through the ages, to know that there is a self-existing King, eternal, immortal, invisible, the only wise God, who alone hath immortality, dwelling in that light which is unsearchable and full of glory; a God who existed when there was no sun, no moon, no stars, no earth nor ocean, no mountains nor fountains abounding with water; that there is an eternal God who is above them all, an eternal God who would continue to be, were all things swept away into their original nothingness; a God having self-existence, having infinite perfection, Jehovah, 'I am that I am; and I am because I am the God that hath life in himself'. Man fell first from his state of innocency from his not being 'still'. Had Eve been 'still' and known this, would she have listened to her tempter? Had Adam been 'still' and known this, would he have listened to any solicitation? Had the tempter been 'still' and known this, would one thought of apostasy have entered his mind? But does not this truth assume a peculiar aspect with regard to us fallen men? This truth, which is the fundamental truth of all religion which meets alike the case of fallen angels, and that of fallen men on earth, and that of saints in heaven (though we fundamentally assume a particular aspect unto us fallen men for the knowing that Jehovah is God) implies in it the knowledge that he hath in himself all that perfection which renders the salvation of lost men possible, and, as we have heard this day, honourable unto him. 'Be still, and know that I am God.' This voice, coming forth from the throne of the Eternal, and ever heard, maketh peace in the high places. The holy angels are 'still', and know that God is God; God is able to uphold them, and therefore a God in whom they have security that they shall never be devils. And as this knowledge is [that by which] Michael and Gabriel know that they shall never be devils, for there is nothing in themselves to hinder but because Jehovah is God, and because they know sufficiently his power and gracious purpose to have confidence in him that he will preserve them; so the hope in men of renewed rectitude, tranquillity and joy when they have been lost is just the farther development of the same knowledge, the knowledge that Jehovah is God.

GOSPEL

Its Invitations Universal

Every man in the world needs this Lamb of God for the taking away of his sin.

Then, considered as exhibited to sinners of mankind in the gospel, it is equally fitted for each sinner of the human race. The gospel is just as much fitted for me as for you, and for you as for me. Christ and his sacrifice just meet your case, as they meet mine. The sinner's need corresponds to what is in the sacrifice of Christ, and what is in the sacrifice of Christ corresponds to the sinner's need.

Again, there is a universal extent of command with regard to its proclamation. We don't yet say, and it is the church's fault in a great measure, that this command in its full extent has been obeyed. In the providential management of its proclamation, alas! how many yet sit in darkness and in the shadow of death externally. But there is a universality of extent in the command, 'Go and preach the gospel to every creature'. There is a command of God that wherever there is a sinner there shall be a setting forth of the Lamb of God, with command to that soul to 'behold the Lamb of God'.

Then, as there is a universality of command to proclaim this gospel to the whole world, and every creature in it, so wherever it is proclaimed it contains a free and unfettered, and universal and special invitation – universal to all, special to each – to look and be saved. It warrants my conscience to cast the weight of my guilt upon the atonement of Christ, to cast the shameful depravity of my nature on the fountain opened for sin and for uncleanness, to cast my whole state as a sinner on Christ the Saviour set forth before me in the gospel. There is this universality which every creature needs: it is to be preached to every creature; wherever it is preached it contains a full and free warrant to every individual to betake himself to the Lamb of God as the only Saviour, with assurance that he shall not be cast out.

The Gospel Warrant

If only convinced sinners are warranted to embrace Christ, then I must, ere I can be warranted to embrace him, be convinced that I am a convinced sinner. But the

Holy Spirit is the only source of infallible conviction, and the Holy Spirit is nowhere promised to convince of conviction; he is only promised to convince of sin. True, the convinced sinner is the only capable subject of saving faith, but it is not as a convinced sinner I am called upon to come to Christ. The gospel does not address convinced sinners as such with offers of reconciliation, but fallen sinners. It is a very beautiful arrangement in the gospel that it does not proclaim itself to convinced sinners. None are so unwilling to consider themselves convinced as those who really are. Every unconvinced sinner imagines himself to be a convinced sinner till the Spirit works in his heart. But the convinced sinner would be the last to embrace an offer made to convinced sinners; but proclaim the gospel to a vile, guilty sinner, and he saith, 'That is I'.

The Sinner's Gospel

Mind, you have got the sinner's gospel, and if you have it, it is to give to sinners; if you have it, you are a debtor to all the sinners to give it to them; and then you have to be very nice, and let the sinners know that you are a sinner too when you give it to them, and that you have nothing else for yourself but that. Let us be sure to give it, lest if we do not give it, we do not get it: lest the Holy Spirit do not give it to us, if we keep it to ourselves. As being saved by the sinner's gospel, God has made us evangelists to the world.

THE HOLY SPIRIT

The Personality and Procession of the Spirit

Three human persons are three human beings; three angelic persons are three angelic beings; three divine persons are *one* Being. The divine Personality must be unique. But except in Hebrews 1:3, the word 'Person' is not used in Scripture – 'Who being the brightness of his glory, and the express image of his Person' – or the effulgence of his glory, the stamp of his Person, the exact correspondence, as the coin corresponds with the stamp which it got in the mint. Still we shall see that the word 'Person', besides that text is an appropriate word. What kind of persons do you call 'I' and 'He'? Personal: Well, 'The Father who sent me, he doeth the works' – the Father is a Person. And Christ calls himself 'I' always: 'I came down from heaven not to do mine own will' – the Son is a Person. The relations of Father and Son are personal relations. Then Christ says, 'I will send you another Comforter that *"he"* may abide with you for ever' – that is a Person, is it not? Then there are the personal properties. Christ is the only begotten Son of God – to beget is a personal property; to be begotten is a personal property. And that which is applied to the Holy Ghost – to be promised, and to come – is a personal property. Christ says, 'The Spirit, which proceedeth from the Father'. The Western Church, Romish and Protestant say, 'From the Father *and the Son* – they introduced that into the Nicene Creed. It is not expressed in so many words in Scripture – the Western Church affirms it, and thinks it has sufficient ground for deducing it as a scriptural consequence. The

Greek and Roman Church, it is there that the doctrinal split is between them – but the doctrine of Rome and the Protestants concerning the Trinity is identically the same. I think Calvin was very well guided when he received the first four creeds. The four creeds are held by the Greek Church as well as the Romish Church, with the exception of these words concerning the procession of the Spirit, '*and from the Son*'. I think the Western Church did wrong in this; they had no right to put an article into the Nicene Creed without calling a Council of the whole Church; yet I think that the article put in is true. The Greeks, some of them, by no means all, denied the truth of the procession of the Holy Spirit from the Son – and others only denied the right to put it into the Creed. The Greek Church explained itself thus: the 'Holy Ghost proceeds from the Father, and *takes* of the Son'.

The Holy Spirit and Scripture

The Spirit of God makes known the things of God, as things given of God to those to whom the Spirit is given to know these. We must observe this enclosing language of Holy Scripture; we must not look beyond, but in the Scripture, and we will find that every passage either proves itself or is proven by parallelism. Hereby we know that we know him, by his Spirit that he hath given to us; the things revealed by the Spirit the apostles spake. God employs human speech; but he himself selects the words that are to express his thoughts. He leaves not man to put words on them; the words are as much the Spirit's as the ideas, and the Apostle Paul studiously avoids other words.

JEWS

Oh, that I could get *any*, *any* Gentile to know the heart of a Jew – but it seems as if I am to get no sympathy (for I do know something of it) but that of my blessed Lord Jesus personally and individually. Yes, thou who wast sent to the house of Israel, who, according to the prophecy of Caiaphas, diedst that the whole people should not perish, who prayedst on the cross, 'Father, forgive them, for they know not what they do', who saidst, 'beginning at Jerusalem', whom thy Father having raised up sent to them first, to bless them in turning every one of them from their iniquities, *Thou*, *Thou*, O crucified King of the Jews! hast from the core of thine own Israel-loving heart put into my heart, whose own flesh they are not (as they were thy Paul's), a burning, burning, burning 'heart's desire and prayer to God for Israel, that they may be saved'. JEHOVAH, God of Israel, thou rememberest with what curdling awe I many years ago read thy dealing with Ezekiel (4:4), and how thou hast brought upon me a little, yet but a little, for I am weak and thou art gracious, thou as much as I can bear, and more than I could bear, were I not strengthened by the Spirit. Oh! these words lie heavy: 'Therefore the wrath is come upon them to the uttermost'. But alas! It seems 'nothing to all that pass by'.

Poor synagogue! There is no pagan image there – no triple-crowned Man of Sin – nor the devastating sword of Isaac's brother. Moses is there, the prophets are there; 'but the name of Jesus is not there', the Spirit of God is not there. Only among the echoes from the distant past sound sadly on the ear of the Christian visitant the mournful words of Israel's Holy One, once great in the midst of thee, 'Woe also unto you when my Spirit departeth from you!' Departing, being resisted, grieved, quenched, yet meaning to return, at the time to us unknown, which infinite wisdom hath fixed in the divine chronology, he hath left behind a book of his own inspiration. Yonder antique roll so reverentially guarded, so solemnly unfolded – it is the law of Moses the servant of the Lord – the volume of the book, in which it is written of him, who of old looking on it said, 'Lo, I delight to do thy will, my God, yea, thy *Torah* is in my heart.' Moses still hath in every city them that preach him, being read in the synagogues every Sabbath-day. Him who spake by Moses they still call their Father. But the old complaint remains, with aggravation, 'This people draw near unto me with their mouths, and with their lips do they honour me, but have removed their hearts far from me'. And so rests the veil on Moses' face and on their averted heart. 'O Jehovah, hear us! that people may know that thou art Jehovah, and that thou hast turned their heart back again.' The God of truth hath said, It shall be done; and when their heart is turned to the Lord, the veil shall be taken away. With unveiled face shall they behold the glory of the Lord.

JUSTIFICATION

Justification and Sanctification

Justification and sanctification are confounded, and indeed absolutely identified, by the Council of Trent, section VI, chapter 7: 'Justification itself is not the remission of sins alone, but also the sanctification and renewal of the inner man, by the voluntary receiving of grace and of gifts; whence the man, from unjust, becomes (or is made) just, and, from an enemy, a friend, that he may be an heir according to the hope of eternal life'. These two blessings, thus identified in the teaching of man, are, by the teaching of the Holy Spirit, set before us as distinct things, yet indissolubly connected, which we cannot, without grievous injury to the truth of God, and consequently most awful peril to our own souls, either confound or rend asunder.

'Now I send thee', said Christ to Paul, 'to the Gentiles, to open their eyes, and to turn them from darkness to light, and from the power of Satan unto God, that they may receive forgiveness of sins, and inheritance among them who are sanctified by faith that is in me' (*Acts* 26:17, 18). 'Ye are washed, ye are sanctified, ye are justified, in the name of the Lord Jesus, and by the Spirit of our God' (*1 Cor.* 6:2). 'Christ Jesus is made of God unto us wisdom, and righteousness, and sanctification, and redemption' (*1 Cor.* 1:30).

The indissoluble connection of these blessings consists in their each being parts of that one great and perfect salvation unto which God eternally chose sinners of mankind in Christ Jesus, in their both flowing to us from Christ, and being enjoyed in union to him; and in the circumstance that personal holiness of nature and conduct, whilst it forms a meetness for the eternal glory unto which justifying righteousness entitles us, is itself a production of that grace which reigns through imputed righteousness unto eternal life by Jesus Christ our Lord. Yet they differ in many important respects. God in justification imputeth the righteousness of Christ, without the imputation of which there would exist no righteousness at all, through which grace could reign in the sanctification of the unholy. In sanctification his Spirit infuseth holiness, and enableth the exercise thereof, because justifying righteousness entitles to that eternal life of which true holiness is one main constituent. In justification, sin is pardoned because Christ by his atonement made satisfaction for it. In sanctification it is subdued, because it is a positive evil, unfitting man for happiness in the enjoyment of the holy God. In justification God doth equally free all believers from his avenging wrath, and that perfectly in this life that they never fall into condemnation; for it is impossible that men can be some more and some less justified, since the term justification, and as its contrary condemnation, express the award of a judge proceeding according to law, and none can be justified at all before the righteous Judge of all the earth, but upon the ground of a perfect righteousness – that is, something which perfectly answers all the demands of the law and justice; whilst he who appears in such a righteousness, must, in equity, be exonerated from every charge, and have all blessings of life eternal adjudged to him as his right. Sanctification, on the other hand, as will afterwards appear, is a progressive work, by which the subjects thereof are gradually assimilated to the divine image. In one word, justification consisteth in this – that God, as righteous Judge of all the earth, sustaineth, in our behalf, the obedience unto the death, which Christ, in *his own* person presented unto God in our stead; and sanctification consists in the whole work which God by his Spirit effecteth in our persons, as having right thereunto through merit of that obedience.

LAW

Mount Sinai and Mount Zion

Jehovah he is the God. He is a wonderful God, he is a wonder-working God. God quickens the dead, opens the blind eyes, and unstops the deaf ears; and the quickened soul has a voice wherewith to respond to the call – 'Call unto me, and I will answer thee, and shew thee great and mighty things which thou knowest not'; and the opened ear can hear the voice which says 'Look'; and the opened eye can look.

I have been lately, and methinks I still am, at the foot of *Mount Sinai*; and I heard *a voice*, and the voice spake of wrath; the wrath of God, which is revealed from heaven against all ungodliness and unrighteousness of men. God thundered with his voice – who thundereth with a voice like him? I heard the sound of a trumpet, and the voice of words concerning which the Scripture saith, 'So terrible was the sight, that Moses said, I exceedingly fear and quake.'

And the Lord shewed me *a biography* – a biography written defectively in the memory, which at the best is ever treacherous, but written perfectly in the book of God's remembrance. And the voice said, 'Come and read this biography.' I said, O Lord, how can I read it! 'I have read it,' said God, 'and you must, you must.' And when I had looked, still the voice came, 'Turn thee yet again, and I will shew thee greater abominations than these.'

And not a biography only – he shewed me *a heart*. 'There are seven abominations in a man's heart' – seven being the number for completeness. And my eye was fixed on that with horror. I speak not now of godly sorrow or repentance, but of horror; and with something that is surely worse, with shame. For it was not simply my eye fixed on the heart, but God shewing me his own eye looking on it. 'See thy sin under my eye; see, my eye sees that.' God be merciful to me a sinner!

Now I heard a voice, at first distant and mysterious; but it came nearer, *a still, small voice* publishing peace, proclaiming salvation; a voice which came from *Zion*, the city of our solemnities, the city of our God; a voice publishing peace, proclaiming the salvation which came from Zion; a voice proclaiming, as salvation, so also a Saviour: 'Behold, I bring you good tidings of great joy, for unto you is born in the city of David, a Saviour', and not merely a Saviour, and a Saviour on earth – Immanuel, God with us, God among us, God for us – but a Saviour slain.

Methought then I stood on *Calvary*, and heard these words, 'It is finished.' God said, Look into the heart of Christ, and behold him in his vicarious death. Behold him, and 'know the grace of the Lord Jesus Christ, that, though he was rich, yet for your sakes he became poor, that ye through his poverty might be rich'. The greatest depth of this poverty being not in his incarnation – though that was a wondrous depth – look at it in his death.

Then methought also that God said, Come by the blood to the *mercy-seat*. And I heard a voice speak from the mercy-seat from between the cherubim. And what voice was that? 'This is my beloved Son (not merely with whom, but) in whom I am well pleased, hear him!' said he from the mercy-seat, from between the cherubim. 'The Lord is well pleased for his righteousness' sake,' said he from the mercy-seat, from between the cherubim. 'I, even I, am he that blotteth out thy transgressions, and will not remember thy sins,' said he from the mercy-seat and from between the cherubim. 'Return to me, for I have redeemed thee,' said he from the mercy-seat, from between the cherubim. Sweet invitation to me, a departer, 'Return unto me'; God assigning to the sinner the saving cause – 'for I have redeemed thee'.

Then methought the Lord said, 'I know heart-secrets.' And I said, Lord shew me *a heart which thou knowest.* And methought the Lord shewed me a heart. Whose it was he did not say, and I do not know; but a heart which God knows: he shewed me something of it.

It was a heart into which he had put a *new song.* The soul was making melody, attempting to make melody to the Lord. Where it was I do not know; but I heard it singing about the middle of its song. It had been singing other songs before this. It had been singing, 'What profit is there in my blood when I go down to the pit?' It had been singing the fifty-first Psalm; and Jehovah had put a new song into its mouth; he had done it, and it was trying to sing; and I heard it in the middle of its song. It had been reading Revelation 5, and trying to sing some of its numbers; and now it was at these words, 'For thou wast slain.' And oh, how it was sobbing and breaking with a joyous grief, and a grievous joy! It could not get its song sung, though it would have liked it. Oh, how it faltered when it tried to sing 'and hast redeemed us to God by thy blood'!

It was the song of a soul known to God; and many such there are. It was the song of one to whom much had been forgiven, and who therefore loved much; and many such there are. But it was the song of the chief of sinners; of the one to whom *most* had been forgiven, and who loved *most*.

Yet it *faltered* and made wrong music; it jarred, and there was discord; and it grated on its own ear; and pained it. And God was listening to it; the omniscient God, who knows all things. But the song was presented through and by the Mediator of the new covenant; and if there was discord, it was removed by grace in atoning blood, by the sweet accents of intercession; for it came up as music in Jehovah's ear, melody to the Lord. It was not discord in heaven. I would know, O God, what soul that is! O God, let that soul be mine! And tell me of it. Let it be mine! Put a new song into my mouth; teach me to sing it. Teach me to sing it on earth; and to sing it when earth shall be no more.

Mosaic Law and New Testament Believers

There are three main heads of Mosaic Law:

1. Law Moral, for which there is strictly no theocratic punishment. 'Thou shalt love thy neighbour', etc. If a Jew did not do that, he sinned a sin deserving punishment. But he could not be stoned for it. There was no theocratic punishment.

2. Law Ceremonial, which had a double relation – first, to the law moral; second, to the law judicial. This ordained that sacrifices were to be brought for sin. But these could not atone for *hamartia* [sin]; for Adonai was injured, whenever any of his creatures were injured.

3. Law Judicial, civil jurisprudence . . . Now, how far have we to do with the judicial law? Is it obligatory except

on the Hebrews? Certainly we have not to do with the Mosaic law in its Sinaitic form. There is certainly an abrogation of that. It was but for a time. Yet the moral law of Adonai is eternally obligatory: and in room of the laws of Sinai, we have positive Christian institutions for all time to come. These are the Sacraments of Baptism and the Lord's Supper, which are to remain in the Christian church 'till the end of the eon'.

Law and Liberty

'But whoso looketh into the perfect law of liberty, and continueth therein, he being not a forgetful hearer, but a doer of the work, this man shall be blessed in his deed' (*James* 1:25).

The word 'perfect' is a favourite one with the apostle James. When he exhorts in this chapter to patience, it is, 'But let patience have her perfect work, that ye may be perfect and entire, wanting nothing'. And speaking of the proper regulation of the tongue, in the third chapter, he says, 'If any man offend not in word, the same is a perfect man'. In the text he directs our attention to 'the perfect law of liberty'. We said before that it is usual for men to oppose these two terms one to another – to set law against liberty, and liberty against law. Hence so much of the wickedness and the misery that are in human society – men speaking oppression and revolt. Speaking oppression – law against liberty; speaking revolt – liberty against law. But the apostle conjoins these two thoughts – liberty and law – perfect law and perfect liberty – 'the perfect law of liberty'. This can be only under the wise and good law of a wise and good sovereign, and in its perfection only in the law of God. A perfect law of liberty can be found only under a perfect sovereign with a perfect law – that is, God alone.

And this law – that is, the eternal, immutable law of God, together with all the peculiar acts of the Christian religion, taken in connection with all the doctrines of the blessed gospel, and all the glorious privileges of the children of God – forms a perfect law of liberty; a liberty from the love of sin, from the dominion of sin, from the guilt of sin; a liberty of drawing near to God; a liberty of asking counsel of the Lord; a liberty to walk in God's holy, just, and good law, which is liberty indeed. For it is a wide path – there is plenty of width to exercise all the powers, to occupy all the time, to guide and direct in all relations. It is a wide path, it is exceeding broad; there is plenty to do, plenty of pleasant work. Now the judgment which the renewed man, which the believer, forms of the law is this: 'His commandments are not grievous'. In relation to our fallen state, without power, they were a burden too heavy for us to bear. But Christ, our Redeemer, fulfilled them in our room and stead, left us an example that we should follow his steps, by his Spirit writes the law in our hearts, and puts it in our inward parts. And the judgment which believers form is: 'His commandments are not grievous'; by which is meant that they are the opposite of grievous, or disagreeable: they are sweet – 'sweeter than honey and the honeycomb'; precious – 'more to be desired are they than gold, yea than much fine gold'; they give light – 'Thy word is a light unto my feet, and a light unto my path.' Believers, by privilege, are the children of God, and as obedient children they delight to do their Father's will. Being born of God, not of corruptible seed, but of incorruptible, and made partakers of the divine nature, there is a certain congruity, fitness, accordance, between that nature and the things which God commands; so that to do them is delightful. But it is ever to be kept in mind that law is law, and that the will of God is to be done by the renewed man not simply, nor chiefly, because agreeable to his renewed nature, but because it is the will of God. And yet it is very agreeable to his renewed nature, which in its subordinate place makes his doing of the will of God go so smoothly, flowingly; being oiled, as it were, throughout all its motions by this, that he who commands – who is holy, and just, and good – by his grace has communicated such a heart to him that he delights in the same things as he does, so doing the will of God from the heart.

LOVE

Love and Charismatic Gifts

'Love never faileth: but whether there be prophecies, they shall fail; whether there be tongues, they shall cease; whether there be knowledge, it shall vanish away.' These spiritual gifts have evanished, some of them, at least. They were necessary for the propagation of the Christian faith in these times – a time of infancy, in the midst of unbelieving Jews and a pagan world – a time when there had not been a Christian education from youth, which supplies in the church in great measure the want of many of them. For this and many other reasons, in the wisdom of God, these gifts have evanished.

But faith, hope and love are gracious – these vanish not.

'Now abideth faith, hope, and love.' These vanish not while time is.

But faith and hope do at last vanish. 'We walk by faith, not by sight' – by which the apostle intimates that walking by faith is one thing, and by sight another; and that the time will come, the eternity will come, when we shall walk by sight, therefore not by faith. So with hope – 'We are saved by hope: but hope that is seen is not hope: for what a man seeth, why doth he yet hope for? But if we hope for that we see not, then do we with patience wait for it' – waiting till the desire comes.

'But the greatest of these is love.' There is what Toplady calls 'The Euthanasia' – the happy death of faith and hope. Faith, when perfected, expires; sight takes place. And hope, when perfected, expires; fruition takes place. But love perfected, continues – heaven is the place of perfected love, eternity its duration.

Love for God

In answering the question, 'What is man's chief end?' I pass over the first part mainly with an intellectual approbation of its moral rectitude as a requirement. 'Man's chief end is to glorify God'; while every fibre of my soul winds itself round the latter part, 'to enjoy him forever', with unutterable, sickening, fainting desire. But I pray the Lord my God to circumcise my heart to love the Lord my God, to love him for his own essential, revealed excellencies with devoted love; that the Beloved (O my soul, O Spirit of the Lord, is he or is he not my Beloved?) may be mine, and I his, and I his, and I his.

Love for Others

The command, is not, 'Thou shalt love thyself as thy neighbour', but, 'thy neighbour as thyself'. There is a priority, but a priority among equals. The Talmud says, 'He who says "Mine is mine and thine is thine" is a just man. He who says, "Mine is mine and thine is mine" is a wicked man. But he who says, "Thine is thine and mine is thine" is a good man'. Love seeketh not her own . . . If you are without love, then the church bell is as good a Christian as you.

Two Kinds Of Love

Love is of two kinds – the love of benevolence and the love of delight. The one is without regard to the qualities of those who are loved – without regard to return, without regard to any attractive quality. Such is the love of God and Christ to us – pure benevolence. And it is this which sends out the city missionary, the Christian man, to the outskirts of society, not on account of any good they have, but because of the God they need, which he instrumentally and God effectively can impart. But there is also the love of delight, which is a moral quality. Such is the love of God to his Son, and such also, because of the fruit of his own grace, is the affection of God and Christ. This love, we see, is not blind, it is discriminating – 'it rejoiceth not in iniquity'. To the iniquity as iniquity it cannot extend itself; but in the proclamation of the word of grace God has made provision for evildoers being, by God's grace, turned unto him in true repentance, in newness of heart and life; and thus love can extend, and does extend, even to the workers of iniquity.

But it rejoiceth not in iniquity. It is a false love which is extended to iniquity, which goes out to a man in the way of cloaking and countenancing his iniquity. To love a man and to love his sin, is to love a man and love his ague, to love his fever. I cannot love a man and love his disease – I cannot love a man and love his sin. Yes, but blessed be God, through his grace love has something to give it joy, even in this world, where there is so much sin, and which is for the most part joyless. There is truth – it 'rejoiceth in the truth'. 'Truth shall spring out of the earth, and righteousness shall look down from heaven.' There is truth on earth, God has a people; there are righteous ways of God, and there are men walking in them. There are things by grace taking place in this world in which love can have joy, and it does rejoice, 'rejoiceth in the truth'.

MAN

What is Man?

Here we are, with the heavens above our heads. What are we? Men. How came we to be men? What is man? How came he to be? And to be as he is? We are on the earth, and the beasts can't ask any questions; the heavens are above us, and the eagle soaring into them can't ask any questions. 'In the beginning God created' – man is God's image on earth; man, the divinely-formed microcosm, of the dust of the earth and the breath of God. Dust connects him with this earth, with the whole solar system, with the whole mass of matter, which, so far as we can judge, is a unit. We differ from it *plasmati* [by formation]: God put his hand to us; he made the rest by his Word. We were made in Adam before he sinned; we were therefore connected with God and with the whole world of spirits.

MINISTRY

The Call to the Ministry

Brethren, you will soon be called to the important duty of calling among you one to break the bread of life among you, and to perform amongst you the high functions of the Christian ministry; and allow me, in reference to that, to address to you the same exhortations: 'Behold the Lamb of God'. He is the Chief Shepherd. He has shepherds under him. He has a shepherd for you. I know not, you know not, who he is – he knows himself. He knows, and he is to be consulted. It is your duty not so much to call a minister as if you were the originators of the matter, as to discover and invite him whom the Lord sends. The Lamb of God, who bought the church with his own blood, is to be consulted in this matter. Do not please yourselves or one another; do both, but in their proper place. Inquire of the Lord. 'Behold the Lamb of God.' He is not removed. The under-shepherd may, but the Chief Shepherd yet abideth. He will not leave you as sheep without a shepherd. He knows; consult him, look to him; he will supply you. And in the exercise of judging, this text will give very much of profitable direction to you. Seek a man – this text may guide you – seek a man of the spirit of John, the sum of whose message is, 'Behold the Lamb of God!' ... Beware of any who would give the least manifestation of seeking to lead away disciples after him. Beware of this world's philosophy and of this world's rhetoric. Beware of him who, if not in matter, yet in manner, preaches himself. Look for the man who appears most to have seen, most to be beholding, the Lamb of God, and whose whole address to you points away from himself and all others to behold the Lamb of God.

OBEDIENCE

Returning to God the Only Way to Obey God

If man examines why he disobeys, he will find, universally, that it is from a notion that he will promote his happiness better by disobedience than by obedience. It is distrust of the truth that God makes all things work together for good to them that love him, that lies at the foundation of sinners not loving God; for, say they, 'If we love him we must obey him, and if we obey it would not be so well with us, as if we disobeyed him'. It is distrust of the truth that God makes all things work together for good to them that love him, which leads to the violation of that command: 'Love God with all your heart, soul, mind, and strength', for every man pursues only after that which, in some way or other, he conceives to lead to personal good. It is distrust of Jehovah's goodness that lies at the root of transgression. In short, man ceases to depend upon God for good, and then, depending upon himself, he seeks happiness by transgression. I appeal to all who are able to dissect the operations of their own souls: is this not the case?

A departure, then, of the soul from God, as its supreme good, led the soul of man into disobedience to God's authority, and, seeking to find happiness out of God, he sought it in a way which the law forbids: 'Do everything to the glory of God'. Where the soul seeks for happiness, in any other way it must necessarily oppose the law of God, whose command is first of all, 'Thou shalt love the Lord'. If, therefore, we would have our thoughts and our way completely changed, we must give up seeking our happiness from any other than God himself; we must seek it absolutely and simply in the Lord Jehovah and in his being what he is. This is the beginning and foundation of a new way. We must, first of all, be satisfied that Jehovah, such as he is, be the sole portion of our souls; we must be contented with his being what he is, and it must be blessedness enough unto us that Jehovah is just what he is. Then when the soul seeks no other felicity than the enjoying of God, it will seek no other rule of action than the will of God. When the soul is completely satisfied just to be what Jehovah wishes it to be, there cannot enter into the mind the thought of enjoying God by disobeying God – the thought of becoming like him, which is necessary to the enjoying him, by disobeying him, which is both the having and fostering the possession of a nature contrary to his.

Now, to take men back to God is just what Christ came to do – is just what Christ is proposing in the gospel to do. The question now is proposed in the simplest form. It is not merely, 'Will you go back?' but, 'Would you be willing to be taken back to God?' Jesus did not come to deliver from any thing else than the alienation from God. Jesus came to open men's eyes, to turn them from darkness to light, and from the kingdom of Satan unto God. Those who, by divine grace, received him, turned from idols to serve the living and true God.

Jesus loved his people and gave himself for them; he both redeemed them by his blood, and made them kings and priests unto God. Once they were afar off from God, but now they are brought nigh by the blood of Christ. The blood of Christ sprinkles the conscience from dead works to serve the living God. They who believe in him are God's.

PASSION WEEK

[Dr Duncan looked out of his bed, and observed David Brown's niece, a little girl, who was sitting on the floor, looking at him.] 'Oh, Missy, are you there? What are you at in your Bible lesson at Mr Oliphant's?' 'We've just finished the Passion Week.' 'Oh, lassie, lassie, there was never a week like that since the world began, and there never will be a week like it again: that was the week of weeks – there never in the universe will be a week like that. There are in the heavens a heap of fixed stars, and probably all of them have suns or planets round them; but never in the universe of God did there take place such things as took place that week on this earth.'

PREACHING

Summary of an Assembly Address by Dr Duncan on Preaching the Gospel

Professor Duncan said that in desiring and aiming at the conversion of sinners and the edification of saints, it was of great importance that they should have a distinct idea of what the conversion of a sinner meant. He thought it was, in a great measure, owing to the want of this that a number of those disorders in practice and errors in doctrine, to which Dr Cunningham had referred, might be traced. Next to, and closely connected with, an earnest desire for the salvation of souls, and a constant expectancy (which could not be too strongly inculcated), was the right and scriptural understanding of what they aimed at when they desired and expected a sinner's conversion.

Conversion was not merely to be understood as a turning from one thing to another thing, but as the turning of an absolutely lost sinner to the God of free and sovereign grace. It was therefore of great importance in existing circumstances, and at all times, that their minds and spirits should be under the sober regulation of revealed truth. And while different suggestions had been thrown out as to the means of promoting these ends, one deeply important question for them to consider was, What was the improvement or the amelioration of those means which they were already employing under the authority of the Word of God, which ought to be adopted in their present circumstances? The question was not only, should there be more preaching, but should there be better preaching? Here he begged to refer to the earnest admonition given by Dr Malan at the Assembly in Glasgow, to beware of Arminianism. He (Dr Duncan) did not believe that Arminianism existed in their own Church. But he could not disguise from his own mind, that of late years, at least previous to the Disruption – he knew not how it may have been since, for they could not expect to get rid of all these evils in a day – since evangelism had become more fashionable, it had become more indefinite and diluted; and if this did not amount to Arminianism, it was a rounding off the corners of that which was called Calvinism, but which he believed to be Jehovahism; it was a rubbing off and a smoothing down of the salient points of Calvinistic doctrine into something on which all who were called Calvinistic evangelicals and Arminian evangelicals could agree. Now this was just the beginning of the evil – it was the letting in of waters – the dilution of the gospel; and the dilution of the gospel would very soon lead to the perversion of the gospel. He remembered an anecdote of a poor man and his wife in England, who were labouring people. They attended a dissenting minister, who, in the course of his ministrations, recommended a Commentary on the Bible. These poor people accordingly laboured to be able to purchase one, and were at last able to do this. After perusing it for some time, the man asked his wife what she thought of the Commentary. 'Why,' said the wife, 'we used to read the Bible in the evening, and it seemed to do us good; and now that we have got the Commentary, it is very good, no doubt, but I do not think it does us so much good. The Bible did us good like a glass of wine, but the Commentary does us good like the same glass of wine in a pailful of water.'

Dr Duncan reminded them that zeal for God's glory should be ever uppermost in the minds of his servants. When they urged sinners to repentance, the character and claims of Jehovah should be laid as the basis for it. This was the basis of all revelation – Jehovah, he is God. This was a doctrine not only of the Old Testament, but set forth and explained in the New Testament, where he was set forth as working all things after the counsel of his own will.

The doctrine of man's fall – his total fall, not merely from virtue and righteousness, but his total alienation, from Jehovah, and the consequent loss of all internal good, his entire separation from Jehovah God, out of which came the doctrine that the Fall was a total ruin, ought to be much insisted on. The doctrine, too, of *the Trinity*, ought not only to be referred to, but set forth in their whole preaching, in its relation to the manifestation of God's glory in the salvation of sinners. Their preaching should be the gospel of the triune God. The doctrine of the Trinity should be ever taught, though not ever formally taught. The doctrine of the person of Christ, which gives glory and excellence to the work of Christ, should be brought forward – not salvation merely, but the glorious Saviour himself, and that not only for the sake of guilty sinners' salvation, but for the exhibition of the divine character – that it was worthy of God to save sinners for such a Saviour. Man's total apostasy from God – his total depravity – would lead to the exhibition of what alone could be, in an apostate's condition, any comfort or support – *the love of Jehovah.* It opened such a deep wound that nothing but a Saviour – as a Saviour for an absolute sinner, dead in trespasses and sins – could heal it. God should be proclaimed as the sole Creator, Christ as the entire Saviour, not the Redeemer only, but the quickener also, not the author of faith only, but the perfecter and finisher of faith. The doctrine of *man's impotency*, of his total inability to bring himself back to God, should be held up. The opposite doctrine, the doctrine of man's ability to convert himself, countenanced the absurdity that man was to return to a dependence on Jehovah by the belief of a certain independence; which was not only absurd, but also dishonourable to God.

It would not do to tell a man that he *might* come to Christ, but that he *must* come. Some, indeed, would have man to do all, though he could do nothing; and others would have him to do nothing, because all was done for him: 'As long as I am told that I must come to God, and that I *can* come, I am left to suppose that some good thing or some power of good remains in me, and I arrogate to myself that which belongs to Jehovah. The creature is exalted, and God is robbed of his glory. If, on the other hand, I am told that I cannot come to God, but not also that I must come, I am left to rest contented at a distance from God, I am not responsible for my rebellion, and Jehovah is not my God. But if we preach that sinners *can't* come, and yet *must* come, then is the honour of God vindicated, and the sinner is shut up. Man must be so shut up that he must come to Christ, and yet know that he cannot. He must come to Christ, or he will look to another, when there is no other to whom he may come; he cannot come, or he will look to himself. This is the gospel vice, to shut up men to the faith. Some grasp at one limb of the vice and some at the other, leaving the sinner open – but when a man is shut up so that he must and cannot, he is shut up to the faith – shut up *to* the faith, and then will he be shut up *in* the faith. God is declared to be Jehovah, and the sinner is made willing to be saved by him, in his own way, as sovereign in his grace.'

Many might dislike this doctrine as harsh and severe, but it was because they viewed God's sovereignty apart from his grace. They spoke of the sovereign God, but why not of the sovereignty of grace? For himself, he felt comfort when shut up to this truth, that God was sovereign, and his grace sovereign; for though he was a sinner – an absolute sinner, Jehovah had said, 'I will have mercy on whom I will have mercy.' This doctrine came like heaven's own thunder, and struck down all human dependence. It came upon a man as lost, as the very chief of sinners, and depending solely on God's will; and then, oh, how blessed to know the sovereignty of grace! It struck him down when he read, 'The Son quickeneth whom he will.' His mind fixed on the 'whom he will', and he was undone, because it did not depend on his own will, but on the will of another. But he read again and found that it was the Son that quickeneth whom he will, and this raised him from the dust, because the Son, on whose sovereign will his salvation depended, was the same 'Jesus Christ who came into the world to save sinners, of whom I am chief.'

It was of importance that the truth which gave such glory to God, which alone could comfort, because it alone brought man down, be declared; that Jehovah's glory be exhibited; and that men be made to feel their own emptiness, so that they might see Christ's sufficiency, and Christ's yearning heart over sinners. On what had been said as to the mode of preaching, he should say not a word, as he was sure all were convinced that it was not by might nor by power, but by the Spirit of the Lord. If God gave the desire, and sent his servants forth with his glorious Word impressed on their heart and conscience, he who had given his Word for that very end, would accompany it with demonstration of the Spirit. Having appointed these means, and ordained them, he would give grace to apply them; and he (Dr Duncan) believed that Jehovah had this end in view, and the more so when they were feeling their infirmities and sins.

PROPHETS

To manifest his continued presence in Israel, to renew the proclamation of his name, to denounce his wrath against all ungodliness and unrighteousness, to call for and encourage return and adherence, hope, trust, and obedience, Jehovah raised up from time to time a series of prophets in Israel. Accordingly, the prophetic word ordinarily runs in the following circle – declaration of Jehovah's excellence, recalling to remembrance his grace and wondrous works to Israel, sharp reproofs of their apostasy and sin, threatenings of awful desolating judgments, proclamation of Jehovah's mercy and faithfulness to his covenant, to be manifested in sparing a remnant, and the announcement that finally the days would come when God would perform all the good which he had promised, would send the Deliverer to Zion to turn away iniquity from Jacob, and fill the earth with the knowledge of Jehovah.

PSALMS, PARAPHRASES AND HYMNS

Dr Duncan took up a book of hymns, and read one of Charles Wesley's. 'I wonder how Charles Wesley could write that and be an Arminian. I believe his heart was according to the hymn, and the theology that would have corresponded with it is Calvinism.' *Miss R.:* 'I am glad to sing a Paraphrase sometimes, when I cannot get up to the pitch of the Psalms.' *Dr D.:* 'There must indeed be sincerity in God's worship; but we may sing a Psalm into the exercise of which we are not able at the moment consciously to enter. You are not able to rise to the assurance of the 103rd Psalm, so you will sing the 51st; but are you sure that you can go down to the penitence of it? Some people could pray the whole Lord's Prayer, but the first two words, "Our Father", they stick at them' – *29 June 1867*.

SEMI-PELAGIANISM AND ARMINIANISM

All that is in God is in him infinitely. *Hence* it is that there is no *prosopolepsy* [respect of persons] in him. And hence the difference between the divine and human will – independency being inconsistent with the nature of human will, and predicable only of the divine. Hence also the irrestrictive freedom of grace . . . It is difficult to define the exact shade of difference between the Semi-Pelagian and the Arminian. Semi-Pelagianism, as I take it, affirms the power of nature, with the aid of universally vouchsafed grace, to effect renewal. The Arminianism of Arminius himself, of Curcellaeus, and of Wesley (though not of Episcopius), affirms that no irregenerate man can do that which is spiritually good unless the divine Spirit aids him. But both systems are synergistic. There is a difference, however, between an Arminianising Calvinist and a Calvinising Arminian.

SIN

Confession, Forgiveness and the Lord's Supper

'If we confess our sins, he is faithful and just to forgive us our sins, and to cleanse us from all unrighteousness.' The foundation having been laid, not simply in the Word of God, but laid doctrinally before us this day, in the High Priest over the household of God, and the one offering by which he hath perfected for ever all 'them that are sanctified'; we are here directed by these words into the way of our personal dealing with God on this foundation. 'If we confess our sins, he is faithful and just to forgive us our sins, and to cleanse us from all unrighteousness.' Mark, these words are not to be isolated; it will be pure Socinianism if they are isolated from the High Priest and his one offering; yet in that connection they point out to us the way of our dealing with God through his High Priest as regards the remission of our sins. 'If we confess our sins, he is faithful and just to forgive us our sins.' Ah! sin is easily committed – I say not whether sin is easily forgiven; both are true; the expiation cost so much – but sin indeed is not easily confessed. David is one example. He roared all the day long. He had sung 'The Lord is my Shepherd', and so on. Sweet had been his communion with God, but he had been tempted, had fallen, and had sinned most grievously, both in adultery and murder. And when he had sinned, he would not part from God, and he would not confess to God. If he could have parted with God, he would not have roared, and if he would have confessed to God, he would not have roared; but he would do neither – would neither part with God nor confess to God – and so there was nothing for him but roaring, while his moisture was turned into the drought of summer. God remembered him, sent his prophet and made the king unwittingly condemn himself, and the moment that conviction was carried home, the prophet proclaimed, in the name of God, his absolution.

Still we find in the fifty-first Psalm that he came to God through the High Priest. 'Purge me with hyssop, and I shall be clean: wash me and I shall be whiter than snow.' This is sacerdotal; it is the Priest. He had come to God; nothing would satisfy him but God's own priestly absolution. But we find David saying, in this thirty-second Psalm, 'I said, I will confess my transgressions unto the Lord, and thou forgavest the iniquity of my sin'. Wonderful transaction! 'I said, I will confess.' He roared, and would not confess. Like a son who has grieved and offended his father, and fallen into disgrace, the filial heart was still in him, and the filial heart would not give up his Father, and the pride would not own his sin. But at last, 'I will confess, and thou forgavest'. David was about to make his confession: 'I said, I will confess'; the forgiveness came. Not without confession, but when he said, 'I will confess'. When the heart was open to make a clean breast of it, when he made up his mind to tell God, God waited no longer. He might have waited longer, I do not say before he pardoned, but before he intimated the pardon; but the words 'Thou forgavest' are the language not only of a man forgiven, they are the language of a man who knows that he is forgiven, of a man to whom God has intimated it. So, when he had made up his mind to confess, he was not left to go on with his confession; whatever way it came, when he resolved to call on the Father, there was the indication of his answer. And then David took up the list of sins, and read on; and he read: 'This sin is forgiven, and that sin forgiven, and the next sin forgiven'. The list was read as the list of forgiven sins. Oh, to read over the list of sins committed put into your hand, when what was to be read as a list of debts due to divine justice, is now put into your hand as a list of debts forgiven by divine mercy, debts of gratitude, of binding obligation.

And it is to confirm faith in this forgiveness through the broken body and shed blood of Christ, believing communicants, that you are invited to this Table. By faith of the operation of the Spirit of God, you have been in your measure enabled to receive Christ – I say not, without doubts and difficulties – while salvation in one of its parts, sanctification, is incomplete, these will stand – but with more or less of confidence in the divine grace and mercy, through the High Priest, and his broken body and shed blood alone, you have been enabled to receive Christ Jesus the Lord. You have fed on that body broken and that blood shed, set before you in the word of the truth of the gospel; and to strengthen and confirm faith – not to produce, but to strengthen and confirm it – the Lord has invited you to his Table. That which has been set before you in word, and which faith has received in word, the same is set before you in sign and seal, that it may be received as symbolised and sealed. Yea, for further and more effectual and powerful application, he hath called you to his Table, where he gives you his flesh and blood, both in word explicatory of the sign and seal, and in sign and seal confirmatory of the Word. 'My body', the incarnation of the Word. 'My body broken.' Ah, what a breaking should we have had for ever, had it not been broken!

Its Forgiveness

Thou canst not stand, thou sayest; thou knowest and feelest that thou canst not stand. It is true. But another thing is true too – that there is forgiveness with God. As true as that thou couldst not stand, that none could stand, is it that there is forgiveness with God. And forgiveness with him must be like himself: divine forgiveness, generous forgiveness – just and holy forgiveness, still generous forgiveness. Wouldst thou have it? Thou must go to him for it, it will not be found short of him; it will not be found by any faith of your own that deals with something about him, and not by him, and not with him – even that deals with his Word in any other sense than dealing with himself according to and by his Word. It is with him, therefore return to him. Iniquity is with thee, by it there is no standing for thee; but fall down at his footstool, saying, 'I have sinned, and committed iniquity, and have done wickedly, and have rebelled'. He is saying, 'hearken to me, ye stout-hearted, that are far from righteousness' – I think it is a word you will take if you are at his footstool – 'I bring near my righteousness, and my salvation shall not tarry'.

And hearken to what God the Lord will say, to what voice comes from the mercy-seat: 'I, even I, am he that blotteth out thy transgressions for mine own sake, and will not remember thy sins' – 'I have blotted out as a thick cloud thy transgressions, and as a cloud thy sins; return unto me, for I have redeemed thee.' So let us not set our sin above the forgiveness which is with God. Let us neither deem our sin too little or too great. Too little – as if anything short of all the bowels of divine mercy, all the obedience unto death of the Son of God, and all the riches of divine regenerating and sanctifying grace, were not needed, as if anything short of that were our salvation. Too great, trembling, tempted one, magnifying thy sin needlessly? Don't set thy sin above the bowels of God's mercy, against the merit of the obedience and death of the Son of God; don't set the strength of sin in thee against the almighty power of the Holy Ghost.

Its Deceitfulness

Sin says, 'I'm not sin at all.' Then Sin says, 'I'm pleasant.' Yes, pleasant poison. Then Sin says, 'Ah! do you call that sin? Well, it is but a little sin.' Alas! alas! for us men there can be no little sin, unless there be a little God against whom to commit it. Then Sin says, 'It is a common sin; good people do that.' A good man has crooked legs; are crooked legs therefore no evil? He has stiff joints; are stiff joints therefore no evil? Ah! men don't argue that way about the natural evil, but they do about the spiritual evil because they love sin, and will take any excuse for it, and never readier than when they find it in a good man. Then Sin says, 'If you sin there's Christ to go to.'

SINCERITY

Sincerity No Excuse for Disobedience

'He's at least *sincere*', is a common saying, and in defence of a man whose opinions or actions may be very far astray, and it exonerates the man from the charge of hypocrisy. Of course that is something. It is 'a soul of good' (if you will) 'in things evil'. I doubt not that the present Pope is a very sincere papist; and I believe that Torquemada was a very sincere inquisitor; and some of the scribes and pharisees had a zeal according to the law and 'touching its righteousness' might have been 'blameless'. But that he has acted conscientiously does not prove that a man has done his duty. In other matters, sincerity is not held to be the equivalent of duty. If a man is sincere in his debts, that won't exonerate him. Now, if a man misconstrues what God reveals, though he is sincere in a measure, he is blameworthy to the extent of his light. God has spoken to men in his Word. How would a man take the calling of *his* word in question? He could not tolerate that, but would justly resent it. And though God bear long with us, he must deal with us as a father with suspicious or heedless children. And our not giving heed to what God says is a most serious aggravation of our sin. Its first element is our not *yielding* to him, our want of filial submission. The creature's first duty is to be what God made him. His next duty is to do what God ordains. He is directly responsible for these things. He is only secondarily responsible for inquiry. But the great want in all men who inquire is the want of a simple love of truth, and the want of the 'single eye'.

THEOLOGY

Maintaining the Balance of Truth

A man states a truth which may be one-sided. I state its counter-truth, anxious to escape from the one-sidedness of error. It is a strange thing, that middle station between opposites. It is more than a *juste milieu*. It is the key-stone of an arch, which props the two sides; and sure enough, it is no contradiction, if your *juste milieu* contradicts the two extremes. The key-stone of an arch is not antagonistic to the two sides it supports. Being itself neither one nor the other, it upholds both.

Advice to a Student of Theology

What further advice can I give you? The longer I live the more I am convinced of the importance, especially in these days, when all things, even first principles, are called in question, of maintaining firmly the inheritance which our fathers have gained for us. I am strongly conservative; that retained, progressive also. For we have not exhausted the oracles of God. I have no wish to fetter Christian liberty of thought. We are commanded to prove all things, and hold fast that which is good. The points to which I would especially claim your steadfast adherence are:

1st, The plenary inspiration of Holy Scripture, avoiding, as beyond our knowledge, being out of the field of our experience, all theories about its *modus* [method].

2nd, The true and proper deity of our adorable Redeemer, comprehending the orthodox faith concerning the blessed Trinity.

3rd, The true and proper vicarious sacrifice of Christ on behalf and instead of his people.

4th, Salvation by sovereign and omnipotently efficacious grace.

As means of establishment in these and in all truths, cultivate a deep reverence and fear of God, a deep sense of the infinite evil of sin. Be much in prayer and the study of the Book of God. Receive its teaching as a little child. For its exegesis, think how it would be understood by the foolish things which God hath chosen to confound the wise. 'Trust in the Lord with all thine heart, and lean not to thine own understanding', or that of other men.

Landmarks in Theology

A good way of determining the progressive landmarks of theology might be by selecting typical texts to describe the points made emphatic by the principal teachers of the church. Thus, to take only six. I would connect the name of *Athanasius* with the words, 'Go ye therefore and teach all nations, baptizing them in the name of the Father, and of the Son, and of the Holy Ghost'; *Augustine*, with the words, 'By grace are ye saved, through faith, and that not of yourselves, it is the gift of God'; 'Not by works of righteousness which we have done, but according to his mercy he saved us, by the washing of regeneration and renewing of the Holy Ghost, which he shed on us abundantly'; *Anselm*, with the words, 'Christ suffered for our sins, the just for the unjust, that he might bring us to God'; *Remigius:* 'I am the good shepherd; the good shepherd giveth his life for the sheep. My sheep hear my voice', etc.; *Luther:* 'Knowing that a man is not justified by the works of the law, but by the faith of Jesus Christ, even we have believed in Jesus Christ, that we might be justified by the faith of Christ, and not by the works of the law; for by the works of the law shall no flesh be justified'; and *Calvin:* 'Blessed be the God and Father of our Lord Jesus Christ, who . . . hath chosen us in him before the foundation of the world, that we should be holy and without blame before him in love.'

Three Unities

I have three synthetic unities:

(1) The Trinity in unity: God the Father, God the Son, and God the Spirit.

(2) The dual unity in the person of Christ the God-man.

(3) The manifold unity of the mystical union, Christ and his church.

I am disposed to consider the mystical union as something midway between the incarnation of Christ and the regeneration of his church. It is the connecting link, and therefore neither the one nor the other. It is Christ becoming incarnate to regenerate man, and so commencing the process with his incarnation. Then the mystical union began. From that it dates.

THREEFOLD UNION

By the words of our blessed Lord – 'Neither pray I for these alone, but for them also which shall believe in me through their word; that they all may be one; as thou, Father, art in me, and I in thee, that they also may be one in us' (*John* 17:20, 21) – our minds are directed to that threefold mysterious chain of union in distinction, which connects our salvation with the nature of the eternal God – the union of the distinct persons of the Godhead in the oneness of being, 'Thou, Father, art in me and I in thee' – the union of the two distinct natures of deity and humanity in the person of Christ, who, with human lips saying, 'Father', proclaims himself the only begotten Son of God – the union of distinct persons, Christ and believers, in one church, one body, of which he is the head and they are the members.

EPILOGUE

Ah! Think now of the infinite God
looking down all this time on our babblings in the dark!

BIBLIOGRAPHY

Brown, David. *Life of the Late John Duncan*. Edinburgh, 1872, repr. Free Presbyterian Publications, Glasgow, 1986.

Brown, David. *Pulpit and Communion Table,* Edinburgh, 1874.

Knight, William. *Colloquia Peripatetica.* Edinburgh, 1870; sixth ed., 1907.

Knight, William. 'Dr Duncan of Edinburgh', *The British and Foreign Evangelical Review,* vol. xxii, pp. 128–59, London, 1873.

Marshall, John E. '"Rabbi" Duncan and the Problem of Assurance', *The Banner of Truth,* issues 201–2; 206–8, Edinburgh, 1980–81.

Moody Stuart, A. *Recollections of the Late John Duncan.* Edinburgh, 1872; repr. as *Life of John Duncan,* The Banner of Truth Trust, Edinburgh, 1991.

Sinclair, J.S., ed. *Rich Gleanings After the Vintage from 'Rabbi' Duncan,* Chas. J. Thynne & Jarvis, London, 1925, repr. Free Presbyterian Publications: Glasgow, 1984.

INDEX

Aberdeen xvii–xix, xxi, 70
Anselm 20, 264
Aristotle 130
Athanasius 264
Augsburg Confession 53
Augustine 19, 20, 103, 172, 182, 264

Baxter, Richard 172, 173
Bellarmine, Robert 173
Bengel, J. A. 173
Bonar, Horatius xxviii
Boston, Thomas 173, 174, 176, 177, 179
Boyle, Robert 130
Bradwardine 174
Brown, David xv, xix–xxi, 197, 200, 267
Buchanan, George 123, 174
Budapest, Hungary xxvi, 100
Burns, William C. xxxiv, 57, 174
Bunyan, John 19

Calvin, John 149, 172, 264
Campbell, George 174
Carey, William 70

Carlyle, Thomas 54, 130
Chalmers, Thomas 174, 175
Chrysostom 175
Clark, Adam 175
Coleridge, S. T. 127, 134
Crisp, Tobias 178
Cunningham, William 153, 175, 214, 215
Curcellaeus 256

Delitzsch, Franz 175
Doddridge, Philip 123

Edinburgh xvii, xxvii, xxx, xxxvi, 48
Edwards, Jonathan 132, 176, 177
Episcopius, Simon 256
Erasmus, Desiderius 177
Erastus, Thomas 177

Fenelon 177
Ferme, Charles 177
Foster, John 130
Free Church of Scotland xxvii, 43
Fuller, Andrew 177

Gill, John 6, 98, 178
Glasgow xxv, xxxvi, xxxvii
Goethe, J. W. 131
Gray, Andrew 64, 201

Halyburton, Thomas 19, 91, 178, 183
Hamilton, William 131
Henry, Matthew 178
Hungarian Reformed Church xxvi

Kant, Immanuel 131
Kennedy, John xli, xlii
Kempis, Thomas à 178
Kidd, James 212
Knight, William xvi, xvii, xxxii, 267

Law, William 178, 179
Leighton, Robert 177
Lessing, Gotthold 131
Locke, John 133
Love, John 179
Luther, Martin 20, 103, 149, 179, 264

M'Cheyne, Robert Murray xxvi
Macleod, John xv
Malan, César xx–xxii, 10, 250
Marrow of Modern Divinity 179, 180
Maurice, J. F. D. 132
Mearns, Duncan xviii, xix, 8, 180

Melanchthon 179
Milne, John 180
Milton, John 134
Moderate Party 62
Moody Stuart, Alexander xxiii, xxvii, xxix, xxxi, 111, 180, 267
Morell, J. D. 132
Muir, John 180
Müller, George 181

New College, Edinburgh xvii, xxvii, xxviii, xxxvi
Newman, J. H 181
North, Brownlow 181

Owen, John xxiv, 181, 183

Polycarp 181
Poole, Matthew 181
Pusey, E. B. 182

Reid, Thomas 133
Remigius 20, 264
Robertson, F. W. 182
Rousseau, Jean-Jacques 132
Rutherford, Samuel 160, 182

Sabellianism xix
Saphir, Adolph xxvi
Secession Church xvii, xviii
Shepard, Thomas 183
Shorter Catechism 83, 217, 225
Socinianism 127, 180, 257
Spurgeon, C. H. 9

Taylor Innes, A. xxx
Tennyson, Alfred Lord 134
Toplady, A. M. 93, 243
Torquemada 169, 261
Trent, Council of 233
Twisse, William 174

Watts, Isaac 123

Wesley, Charles 123, 124, 255
Wesley, John 6, 98, 256
Westminster Confession of Faith
     53
Whately, Richard 183
Whyte, Alexander xxvii
Witsius, Herman xxiv, 183
Wordsworth, William 127, 134